GLENCOE

Telephone Techniques

SECOND EDITION

Dorothy Neal
Instructor of Business Education
Sacopee Valley High School
Hiram, Maine

Glencoe
McGraw-Hill

New York, New York   Columbus, Ohio   Woodland Hills, California   Peoria, Illinois

Reviewers

Barbara Davis
L. P. Card Skill Center
Pasadena, Texas

Jimidene Murphey
South Plains College
Lubbock, Texas

Dolores Hofmann
Bryant & Stratton
Rochester, New York

Wanda Samson
Fremont High School
Fremont, Nebraska

Library of Congress Cataloging-in-Publication Data
Neal, Dorothy A.-
      Telephone techniques / Dorothy Neal. – 2nd ed.
            p. cm.
      Includes index.
      ISBN 0-02-802011-1
      1. Telephone in business.   I. Title.
  HF5541.T4N43   1997
651.7'3—dc21

97-26449
CIP

Photo Credits: Cover William Westheimer/The Stock Market; **1** T. Kevin Smyth/The Stock Market; **28, 29, 42** Doug Martin; **54** Michael A. Keller Studios Ltd./The Stock Market; **59, 60** Mark Burnett; **80 (l)**David DeLossy/Image Bank, **(c)** Strauss/Curtis/The Stock Market,**(r)** Alan Becker/Image Bank; **90** Alan Becker/Image Bank; **96** David DeLossy/Image Bank; **103** Doug Martin; **116** David Dennison; **123, 125, 126, 127, 128, 130** Doug Martin; **148,** Mark Burnett.

Telephone Techniques, Second Edition

Send all inquiries to:

Glencoe/McGraw-Hill
936 Eastwind Drive
Westerville, OH 43081

ISBN 0-02-802011-1

1 2 3 4 5 6 7 8 066 04 03 02 01 00 99 98 97

Table of Contents

Preface

The telephone is a vital tool for communication within our local areas and in the larger, global environment. We use the telephone daily to communicate with business associates and on a personal level. Communicating over the telephone can be a challenge when the other person is not in view. Thus, we need to develop telephone communication skill that is effective and positive when dealing with the public.

Telephone Techniques, Second Edition, will guide you to learn proper telephone use. The techniques you will study will help you develop and maintain professional relationships, a positive image for your company, and reliable service for your customers. *Telephone Techniques, Second Edition,* consists of a text-workbook, an instructor's manual and key, and a videotape.

Text-Workbook The text-workbook is divided into six chapters that focus on the following topics:

Chapter 1: Developing Positive Telephone Communication Skill

Chapter 2: Processing Incoming Calls

Chapter 3: Making Telephone Calls

Chapter 4: Managing Special Telephone Calls

Chapter 5: Customer Service on the Telephone

Chapter 6: Using Telephone Equipment and Technology

Each chapter opens with objectives, followed by an in-depth discussion of techniques related to the chapter focus. Notes in the margin contain important points and reminders. The sections with a colored background contain useful information that you may want to refer to repeatedly, especially on the job. The video icon appears beside many major topics to let you know these concepts are reinforced in the video.

video icon

The chapters contain numerous activities, as well as some self-assessments, to reinforce what you have learned. Material at the end of chapters includes a summary, one or more reinforcement applications, and a case study.

Videotape A 40-minute videotape reinforces the concepts presented in the text-workbook. The video is divided into four parts:

Part 1: Developing Positive Telephone Communication Skill

Part 2: Processing Incoming Calls

Part 3: Making Telephone Calls

Part 4: Customer Service on the Telephone

Worksheets are available to support the concepts covered in the video and to encourage learning through group discussion. Your instructor may choose to use the worksheets, which are found in the Instructor's Manual and Key, as class activities.

Enjoy using *Telephone Techniques, Second Edition.* With your constant attention and practice, you will develop positive telephone communication skill that you will use lifelong.

—*Dorothy A. Neal*

This book is dedicated to Dr. G. W. (Jim) Maxwell, a long-time professional colleague, friend, mentor, and author. His outstanding telephone skills demonstrate excellence in all aspects of communication, especially his attentive listening. Thank you for your inspiration and support during the writing of *Telephone Techniques, Second Edition.*

—*Dorothy A. Neal*

Developing Positive Telephone Communication Skill

OBJECTIVES

Chapter 1 will help you:

1. Understand the importance of developing positive telephone communication skill.

2. Reinforce the importance of all aspects of communication skills, especially listening.

3. Ask effective questions when you are using the telephone.

4. Integrate the stages of a telephone call effectively for positive telephone communication.

5. Evaluate your own telephone skills and focus on specific areas that need improvement.

A s technology advances, the telephone continues to be an important communication tool. It is used in nearly every business for a variety of reasons.

The world increasingly communicates by way of the telephone. Because of this, the need for strong telephone skills has never been more important. Learning how to refine your telephone skills can improve communication and goodwill in business. By evaluating your overall telephone skill and determining the areas that need improvement, you may develop more purposeful calls and achieve better communication via the telephone.

Your voice is you! Always speak positively.

ASSESSMENT 1: Assessing Your Telephone Skills

How good are your telephone skills? Complete the checklist below, trying to be as objective as you can in assessing your telephone skills. Keep in mind that the ultimate goal is to improve your telephone skills.

	Always	**Usually**	**Seldom**
1. I feel in complete control of every telephone call I make.	_____	_____	_____
2. I answer the phone in a pleasant manner, always identifying myself.	_____	_____	_____
3. Before I begin the call, I have the necessary materials in front of me.	_____	_____	_____
4. I use effective questioning skills.	_____	_____	_____
5. The tone of my voice is pleasant.	_____	_____	_____
6. I try to practice active listening.	_____	_____	_____
7. I screen calls, when necessary, in a professional manner.	_____	_____	_____
8. I never leave callers on hold without getting back to them shortly.	_____	_____	_____
9. I use message forms for completing messages when appropriate.	_____	_____	_____
10. I use telephone directories to assist me in preparing for calls.	_____	_____	_____

11. I am sensitive to international
time zones when making calls. _____ _____ _____

12. I use various telephone options,
such as call forwarding and
call waiting, when appropriate. _____ _____ _____

THE COMMUNICATION PROCESS

Assume that you need feedback from a coworker who is a team member on a very important project. You phone her and she answers immediately, but you sense by the tone of her voice that she is in the middle of a problem. When you ask whether this is a good time to speak with her, she replies that she will call you back shortly. Then you hang up.

What role does communication play in this situation? The tone of your coworker's voice has sent you a verbal cue that a problem exists and this is not a good time to speak with her. You have demonstrated sound listening skill and good judgment by responding quickly to the tone of her voice.

Communication is the process of exchanging ideas and messages either verbally or nonverbally. Communication consists of four major parts: speaking, reading, writing, and listening—with listening being the most important. Figure 1-1 shows the process of communication. Using the telephone requires you to verbally communicate a message or to receive a message. When a message is not conveyed as it is intended or is not interpreted as it should have been, miscommunication occurs. Practicing each part of communication conscientiously will help you avoid miscommunication.

Figure 1-1 The four segments of the communication process interact.

Much communication is visual, and you look at the other person for clues about the message. Is the person looking you straight in the eye? How is the person dressed? What does the expression on the person's face tell you? Communicating on the telephone, however, differs from communicating face-to-face: you cannot see the other person or party. Since you have no visual clues to understand, you can only listen to the speaker's voice. The person to whom you are speaking also depends on you to speak in a way that will enable both of you to understand. The fundamental skills of speaking and listening are important to prevent any miscommunication or confusion.

ACTIVITY 1: Communicating Without Seeing

The purpose of this activity is to help you understand the effect of not being able to see someone with whom you are communicating, which happens when you are talking on the telephone. Select a partner for this activity. Turn your backs to each other, and have a short conversation about the best thing that has happened to each of you thus far today. After you have completed that conversation, turn around and face each other. Then, talk to each other about the worst thing that has happened to each of you today. After you have completed this activity, answer the following questions.

1. Was it easier to communicate when you were back-to-back or face-to-face? Why?

   _____

   _____

   _____

   _____

   _____

2. What voice clues did you use to help you understand what your partner was saying when you had no visual contact?

   _____

   _____

   _____

   _____

3. What visual clues did you use to help you understand what your partner was saying when you were face-to-face?

   _____

   _____

_____

_____

_____

4. What did you learn about communicating with no visual contact that will assist you when you are using the telephone?

_____

_____

_____

_____

SPEAKING

When you speak on the telephone, you cannot use your appearance, posture, eye contact, and gestures to help convey your message. Your voice must do the job.

A good voice is pleasant to listen to because it communicates a positive message. Keep in mind the following qualities of a good voice:

Appropriate Volume Speak so that your voice is neither too loud nor too soft. Use changes in volume to emphasize important information.

Comfortable Rate Speak slowly enough so that the listener has a chance to absorb your message without your having to repeat it. Keep in mind that as you speak the other person may be writing notes.

Correct Pronunciation and Enunciation **Pronunciation** is the correct way to say a word. **Enunciation** is the clarity with which you speak. To avoid mispronouncing words, you may wish to check the pronunciation of unfamiliar words in the dictionary before you use them. Enunciate your words clearly as you speak.

Be aware that people with an accent or dialect unlike yours may not understand your pronunciation of some words.

People with an accent or dialect unlike yours may not understand your pronunciation of some words. You also may not understand the pronunciation of some of their words. In these instances, careful pronunciation and clear enunciation are very important for effective communication. You may need to repeat or spell words that are unusual or misunderstood.

The purpose of this activity is to reinforce the importance of pronouncing and enunciating words correctly. Select a partner for this activity.

Section 1

Read aloud the following list of words while your partner listens for correct pronunciation and enunciation of each word. Then reverse roles.

1. library
2. Amarillo
3. message
4. affect
5. comparable
6. compromise
7. laboratory
8. hoarse
9. experience

After both of you have completed Section 1, evaluate your overall pronunciation and enunciation techniques. In which areas did you make note of needed improvement?

Section 2

List below five words that you have difficulty pronouncing or enunciating. Use a dictionary to check the pronunciation of the words, if you wish. Practice saying each word aloud until you pronounce and enunciate it correctly.

1. _____
2. _____
3. _____
4. _____
5. _____

Positive Tone With a Pleasant Pitch The **tone** of your voice conveys your attitude, or manner of expression, in speaking. **Pitch** refers to the variation in your voice. It is difficult to listen to people with high-pitched, low-pitched, or monotonous voices. Vary the pitch of your voice in order to make it interesting and pleasant to hear.

SPEAKING TECHNIQUES

Stay Alert. Focus on the telephone call; it is easy to be distracted by what you see around you. Pay attention to what you say and to what is being said to you.

Speak Directly Into the Telephone. Hold the mouthpiece of the telephone an inch or two directly in front of your lips. Speak clearly and friendly, smiling as you speak. Keep objects such as gum, food, and pens or pencils out of your mouth.

Adjust Your Volume. Speak so that the listener can easily hear you. The quality of telephone connections can affect the listener's hearing level. You may need to speak more loudly or more softly accordingly.

Listen to Yourself. Be aware that certain factors can affect your voice. If you have a cold, you may have a nasal sound in your voice. If you are upset, you may speak faster. If you have an accent or a distinct dialect, you will need to speak slowly enough for the listener to understand.

Figure 1-2

READING AND WRITING

Another important part of telephone communication is being able to read, record, and interpret telephone messages successfully. You should ALWAYS be prepared to record any information that may be needed for future reference. Write messages clearly so that they can be read quickly and responded to appropriately. (Reading, writing, and interpreting messages will be covered in greater detail in later chapters.)

LISTENING

Although the four parts of communication must work together, none is more important than listening when you are using the telephone. Think about the last time you used the telephone. How much of that time did you spend listening?

The saying that "Many hear but few listen" is very true. Listening combines both physical and mental skill. It also implies that you heard what someone said and you understood by responding.

The Listening Process Listening involves four related steps: sensing, interpreting, evaluating, and responding.

- *Sensing* means you are aware that someone is saying something to which you need to listen. If sensing does not occur, the listening process never begins.

Stay focused when listening.

- *Interpreting* involves identifying what is said and explaining the speaker's meaning. Although you may hear the words, you can inaccurately explain the message if you do not understand the words as the speaker intended. Because individuals think differently, care must be given to avoid misinterpreting a message. Your knowledge, personality, experiences, and personal interest in the subject all influence how well you interpret what you hear.

- *Evaluating* forces you to think about the whole message and draw conclusions about the content and the way in which you will respond.

- *Responding* requires you to make a statement verbally. Study Figure 1-3 to see how the four related steps are integrated.

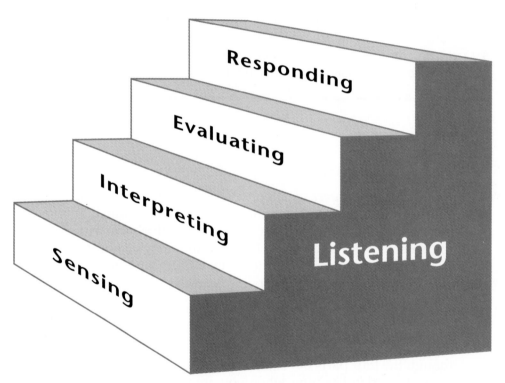

Figure 1-3 Accurate listening is based on the four interdependent steps of the listening process.

Active Listening When you use the telephone to communicate, you must practice active listening. Active listening means that you hear words and thoughts, then respond to them. For example, if you are asked a question during a telephone conservation, you are expected to give a response. The need to respond to the question gives you a particular reason for listening.

ACTIVITY 3: Listening Skill

The purpose of this activity is to help you focus on your listening level when using the telephone. Read and respond to each statement by placing a check mark in the appropriate column. Try to be honest about your current level of listening when you are using the telephone.

	Always	Sometimes	Never
1. I try to listen for facts.	_____	_____	_____
2. I try to concentrate on main ideas.	_____	_____	_____
3. I try to give appropriate feed-back.	_____	_____	_____
4. I try to always be prepared to listen when I am using the telephone.	_____	_____	_____
5. I take notes.	_____	_____	_____
6. I avoid distractions.	_____	_____	_____
7. I ask questions when nec-essary.	_____	_____	_____
8. I avoid making premature conclusions.	_____	_____	_____
9. I try to avoid interrupting the other party.	_____	_____	_____
10. I try to practice telephone courtesy.	_____	_____	_____

Total the check marks in each column. Strive to improve your listening level so that you can answer "always" for each of the above experiences. Remember, all your listening experiences on the telephone should be positive experiences.

Why do people not listen as well as they should when using the telephone? Many have never learned to listen to conversations. They may have different interests or limited knowledge. Often they may model their telephone listening skill after coworkers or others whom they have heard speaking.

As you improve your listening skill, you will become more knowledgeable. In addition, you will gain confidence in dealing with people and difficult or sensitive situations. Improved active listening skill can result in improved work performance and an increased sense of self-worth. Try to always keep a positive attitude recognizing that everything you hear may not be positive.

ACTIVITY 4: Positive and Negative Telephone Talk

The purpose of this activity is to help you evaluate comments spoken over the telephone as being positive or negative. Place a check mark in the Positive *column if you think the comment is positive, or in the* Negative *column if you think it is negative. Be prepared to justify your answers. If possible, read these comments aloud with a partner. Notice how using different tones of voice positively and negatively affect listening when you are using the telephone.*

	Positive	Negative
1. "When will you make a decision about whether you will go to the conference? Don't you think it is about time you did?"	_____	_____
2. "The Advertising Department must have quoted you the wrong price. Hold on, I'll transfer you."	_____	_____
3. "Our records show that your balance is $5329.10. When do you plan to make a payment or let us know how you plan to pay the balance?"	_____	_____
4. "It will be a pleasure to speak at the meeting in Omaha on March 23. I'm thrilled you invited me."	_____	_____
5. "Please don't shout at us. We were not responsible for that decision."	_____	_____
6. "I absolutely will not do as you requested. That is a ridiculous idea."	_____	_____

7. "Why doesn't someone speak to her about her constant habit of interrupting whenever someone else is speaking?" _____ _____

8. "Thank you for calling. I am glad we could be of service to you." _____ _____

9. "He never listens to anything anyone tells him. He is so headstrong. This could be disastrous for him at performance review time." _____ _____

10. "Would you explain the situation to me, please?" _____ _____

When you are making or receiving a telephone call, be ready to listen when you pick up the receiver. While the buzz, beep, or ring of the telephone may distract you before you answer the phone, try to focus your thoughts on the conversation. You would not want to miss important information at the beginning of a call, such as the caller's name, because you were listening for other details.

LISTENING ROADBLOCKS

You may encounter listening roadblocks such as *distractions, interruptions,* or *disconnected* calls. These roadblocks often occur without you even realizing or anticipating them. To deal with these roadblocks that may occur when using the telephone, prepare for them and learn to manage them.

ACTIVITY 5: Interference With Telephone Listening

The purpose of this activity is for you to analyze your telephone listening skills and become aware of what interferes with your telephone listening. Place a check mark beside any of the items below that interfere with your telephone listening.

_____ 1. Noise can be heard on the telephone line.

_____ 2. The caller does not respond or acknowledge comments.

_____ 3. The person being called keeps repeating the same message.

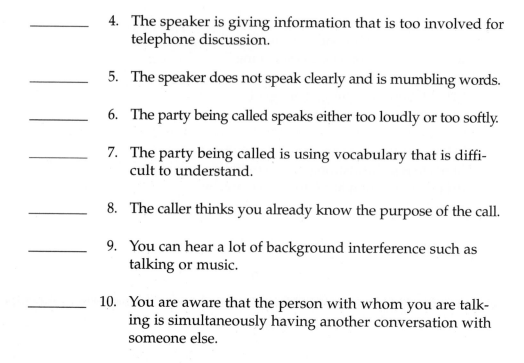

_____ 4. The speaker is giving information that is too involved for telephone discussion.

_____ 5. The speaker does not speak clearly and is mumbling words.

_____ 6. The party being called speaks either too loudly or too softly.

_____ 7. The party being called is using vocabulary that is difficult to understand.

_____ 8. The caller thinks you already know the purpose of the call.

_____ 9. You can hear a lot of background interference such as talking or music.

_____ 10. You are aware that the person with whom you are talking is simultaneously having another conversation with someone else.

Distractions Most of us work with other people; thus, there will most likely be movement, people talking, and noise all around. Some activity and sounds will be loud or unusual. Others, such as the sounds of printers, keyboards, or soft music, blend into the background. Still other distracting sounds may come from the telephone itself if the connection is poor.

How can you handle these distractions if they occur during a phone conversation? You can ask people to be quiet. If movement or activity is bothering you, try turning your back to it or looking down at your desk rather than around the office. This will help you concentrate on the conversation. If a poor telephone connection is interfering with your conversation, explain this to the other person and offer to call back.

Occasionally, your call may be so important that quiet surroundings are necessary. If this is the case, try to find a telephone in a more private location.

Interruptions Interruptions are very annoying when you are talking on the telephone. Often someone will start talking to you or ask you a question when you are on the phone. That person forces you to turn your attention from the call to him or her. Meanwhile, the person on the telephone wonders why you have suddenly stopped talking or responding.

If someone tries to speak with you while you are on the phone, use a signal that indicates you are unavailable at the moment. Put a finger to your lips to indicate "silence, please," or raise your hand in a stop signal. If this does not work, excuse yourself from the call and tell the interrupter that you are in the middle of a call and will have to talk to him or her later.

When you return to the telephone, be sure to thank the other person for waiting.

Disconnected Calls Disconnected calls may be caused by storms, over-loaded circuits, or power failures. Often someone may accidentally press the wrong button on the phone.

If you disconnect a call, immediately place the call again. If you disconnect a call from a person whose telephone number you do not know, wait for that party to call you. If the cause of the disconnection is unclear, then normally the party who initiated the call should call again. When you call back, simply say, "I'm sorry, we were disconnected."

ACTIVITY 6: Dealing With Distractions

The purpose of this activity is to help you learn options for dealing with distractions. Read each scenario below and respond to the questions.

Scenario: Cindy works in a busy office area with seven other team members. Team members walk around her desk talking frequently, even when Cindy is on the telephone. Even worse, one of her team members plays a radio that is tuned to a talk show. Of course, Cindy has a very difficult time concentrating.

1. What can Cindy do about the level of noise and activity taking place around her desk?

   _____

   _____

   _____

   _____

   _____

   _____

2. How should Cindy handle the person who plays the radio?

   _____

   _____

   _____

   _____

   _____

   _____

3. What actions can Cindy take to improve her concentration when she is using the telephone?

_____

_____

_____

_____

_____

_____

OVERCOMING LISTENING ROADBLOCKS

1. When you make a call, find a place where there will be no loud voices or other loud interference. If an interference occurs during a call, excuse yourself from the telephone conversation; then ask the other people to be quiet. In extreme situations, find another phone to use.

2. Keep your emotions in check. Remain objective at all times and be aware of certain situations, words, or individuals that tend to trigger emotions when you are using the telephone.

3. Ask meaningful questions. (Questioning will be covered in detail on pages 20–22.)

4. Practice patience and courtesy at all times. A pause in the telephone conversation does not mean a breakdown has occurred in the discussion. Clarification may be needed.

5. Be prepared to actively listen whenever you pick up the telephone.

6. Listen for specific information. Irrelevant information can cause you to forget the main part of the message.

7. Ask for information to be repeated if you did not understand it.

8. Use the information as soon as possible or record the information for later reference.

9. Use interjections throughout the telephone conversation. By saying "I understand" or "yes," you are demonstrating to the other party that you are listening.

10. Practice listening with coworkers, friends, and relatives. If you practice good listening skills, you can improve them.

LISTENING TECHNIQUES FOR IMPROVED TELEPHONE SKILL

Be ready to listen. Focus on the speaker and the situation. If you are daydreaming or trying to do something else while speaking on the telephone, you are not ready to listen. Keep note-taking supplies handy.

Concentrate. Distractions interfere with the listening process. If you are thinking of other things you have to do, it is easy to lose concentration on what is being said to you or what you are saying over the telephone.

Speak directly into the mouthpiece of the telephone. Use a pleasant voice and clear pronunciation and enunciation.

Be enthusiastic. This conveys a positive image of both you and the business you represent.

Listen for details and key words. By listening for details and key words, you will be able to comprehend the message faster and better.

Ask questions when necessary. If the situation calls for a response, be ready to ask questions when the opportunity arises. Allow the speaker to finish a statement, and then ask the question. Repeat the speaker's ideas in your own words to make it easier for you to remember what was said.

STAGES OF A TELEPHONE CALL

The saying "You never get a second chance to make a good first impression" is especially true when it comes to using the telephone. Whether you are making or receiving a call, practicing good telephone skills allows you to make a great "first impression."

Courtesy and *professionalism* are the bench marks of positive telephone skills. When you are courteous, you are considerate of the people with whom you are communicating. When you are professional, you communicate in a way that creates a sense of satisfaction for both parties.

Every telephone call you make can be compared to a play in which you are a major actor. It would be wonderful if all play performances were outstanding, but some performances are better than others. Likewise, you are always on stage to complete a telephone call courteously and professionally.

Telephone calls can be divided into three stages: the introduction, the purpose, and the conclusion. All three stages are equally important to a successful call.

Attitude is everything on the telephone—keep a good one!

THE INTRODUCTION

Whether you are making or answering a call, the first few seconds of the call are very important. During this *introduction* phase, the parties should be identified and the convenience of the call established. These telephone courtesies should ALWAYS be observed!

Identifying Yourself and the Other Party   Answer the telephone promptly, at least by the second ring, identifying yourself pleasantly. See the examples that follow:

When you answer your own telephone, say:

"Lorine Vergaard speaking."

When you answer a department telephone, say:

"Customer Service; this is Clyde Wolczyk."

When you answer for a firm, say:

"Good morning, Commissioner's office. This is Sunitha speaking."

When you answer another person's telephone, say:

"Dr. Brown's office; this is Brenda."

When you make a call and the other party answers the telephone with a greeting and an identification, immediately identify yourself and your employer, if appropriate.

Caller: "Hello, this is Anna Dearborn from the Cornish Chamber of Commerce."

Recipient: "Hello, Ms. Dearborn. This is Sophia Davis."

If the other person does not identify himself or herself, or if you did not hear the name clearly, courteously ask the name.

"May I have your name, please?"

"Excuse me. Would you please spell your last name?"

"I would be happy to help you. May I ask who is calling?"

If it is necessary to put the caller on "hold," periodically ask the caller if he or she wishes to continue "holding" or to leave a message. If the person being called is unavailable, take a message instead of keeping the caller on hold. (Message-taking will be covered in Chapter 2.) Nothing can ruin customer satisfaction or credibility more than being placed on "hold" for long periods of time. A call might be similar to the following:

Caller: "May I speak with Ms. Parker?"

Recipient: "Please hold; I'll check if she is in her office." (*pause*)
"Ms. Parker is not available at this time. Could I take a message?"

Establishing the Convenience of the Call   When you make a telephone call, you have no idea what the recipient was doing prior to your call. Your call may interrupt an important activity. Therefore, unless your call is an emergency, make sure that the recipient has time to talk with you. Establish the convenience of the call, particularly if it is an international call or a long-distance call involving different time zones. For example, you might say:

"Is this a convenient time for us to speak?"

"May I have a few moments of your time?"

Using these phrases gives the person receiving the call a chance to reply politely whether it is a convenient time to speak.

What do you do if someone calls you, interrupting an important task that you cannot set aside, and immediately launches into the business of the call? If this happens, wait for the person to pause. Indicate that the immediate moment is inconvenient for you to talk and offer to return the call.

"Could I call you back in a few minutes, Courtney? I need to finish the project I am working on."

"Mr. Alawi, I have a meeting to attend. May I call you back this afternoon?"

ACTIVITY 7: Courteous and Professional Communication

The purpose of this activity is to help you develop an awareness for courteous and professional procedure at the beginning of a telephone call. Read each statement and determine if it is courteous and professional. If it is, place a check mark in the Yes *column. If it is not, place a check mark in the* No *column; then rewrite the statement to make it courteous and professional.*

	Yes	No

1. **Caller (Mr. Lord)** "Is Elizabeth Waters there?"

   _____   _____

   _____

   _____

   _____

2. **Caller (Arlene Blake, Human Resources):** "Hello, Mr. Lyons. This is Arlene Blake from Human Resources."

   _____   _____

   _____

   _____

   _____

3. **Receiver (Jane Stevens, Customer Service):** "Customer Service."

_____ _____

_____

_____

_____

4. **Receiver (John Spisak, Shipping and Receiving):** "I can't talk now. I'm in the middle of something more important."

_____ _____

_____

_____

_____

5. **Caller (Louise Stone):** "Good morning. May I ask who this is?"

_____ _____

_____

_____

_____

6. **Receiver (Darrell Chin):** "Who is this? I can't hear you."

_____ _____

_____

_____

_____

THE PURPOSE

After you have exchanged introductory courtesies, establish the _purpose_ of the call. One person needs something from the other; otherwise, the call would not have been made. During this stage of the call, communicate your needs clearly and make sure you understand the other person's needs as well. Do this by expressing your needs, asking questions, and confirming what you are hearing.

Expressing Your Needs   Usually the person placing the call is the one who wants something. That person should state the problem or request clearly and politely, and then give the other party a chance to respond. For example:

> "Could you tell me the colors and sizes these shirts come in? I lost my catalog."

"Would it be possible for me to set up an appointment to speak with Mr. Gamarsh concerning the textbook account?"

"We are having a problem with our copier and would like to have it serviced as soon as possible."

Express what you want in a firm, courteous manner. Do not be rude. Avoid being submissive.

Rudeness: "This stupid copier is broken again!"

Submissiveness: "I'm sorry to have to bother you, but I think we've done something wrong with the copier; it's just not working right."

ACTIVITY 8: Expressing Needs Over the Telephone

The purpose of this activity is to practice expressing your needs as directly as possible when you are using the telephone. Read each statement below and write a statement to express your needs in a courteous and professional manner.

1. You want to order five boxes of computer paper. The boxes MUST be delivered within two days.

   _____

   _____

   _____

2. You ordered seven boxes of staples, but received seven boxes of paper clips.

   _____

   _____

   _____

3. You need to see Jean Simard for approximately one hour within the next two days.

   _____

   _____

   _____

4. You have tried unsuccessfully to reach Mr. Callahan on the phone for three days. You need to see him sometime today in order to finalize a project before the deadline.

   _____

   _____

   _____

5. Because of an emergency, you are calling to reschedule an appointment.

_____

_____

_____

Open questions require more of an answer than yes *or* no *and usually begin with* who, what, where, when, why, *and* how.

Questioning Over the Telephone Ask questions to obtain information. The information may help you answer the other party's request or clarify a response to your needs. Creative questions will yield positive results. Three basic types of questions help you obtain information.

Open Questions. Open questions require more than a *yes* or *no* answer; for example:

"How may I assist you?"

"What date is convenient for us to meet for lunch?"

"What seems to be the problem with the printer?"

These questions require more information and detail. Open questions usually begin with *who, what, where, when, why,* and *how.*

Closed questions can be answered with yes *or* no *and often start with* are you, do you, can, could, did, will, *and* would.

Closed Questions. Closed questions can be answered with a *yes* or *no* answer. For example:

"Would you like to order the blue labels?"

"Will you be available at 4 p.m. on Friday?"

"Is the machine transmitting?"

Closed questions are used to verify information. They often start with the words *are you, do you, can, could, did, will,* and *would.*

Forced-choice questions require an either-or *response.*

Forced-Choice Questions. Forced-choice questions require an *either-or* response. You give the listener a choice of two or more options from which to select. For example:

"Would you prefer us to meet you at The Lobster Pot Restaurant at 12:30 p.m. or 12:45 p.m. for lunch?"

"Would you care to place your order today or tomorrow?"

Formulate your questions carefully in order to obtain pertinent information.

The purpose of this activity is to identify the three major types of questions and develop an awareness for using a particular type of question when using the telephone. Identify each question as open, closed, or forced-choice. *Know why you made your choice.*

_____ 1. What did you do with the telephone number I gave you?

_____ 2. Have you paid for the tickets to the concert?

_____ 3. Should I send the final check to the old address or the new address?

_____ 4. For what type of position are you interested in applying?

_____ 5. Why do you think the supplier will miss the delivery date?

_____ 6. Do you plan to tour the new plant when you are in Boston?

_____ 7. Those were very high standards, weren't they?

_____ 8. Why wasn't it possible to record that information?

_____ 9. Can it be repaired within two days?

_____ 10. Would you prefer to purchase $100,000 or $150,000 worth of coverage?

_____ 11. Did your supervisor tell you the whole story?

_____ 12. How many calls did we log yesterday?

SUGGESTIONS FOR POSITIVE QUESTIONING

Listen attentively to all questions. Use those questions in order to rephrase your own questions to get the result you desire.

Pay attention to how questions are phrased and the words used to begin the question. This helps you focus more closely on the answer you may give.

Jot down the major questions you want to ask. By doing this, you will feel more confident and in control of the questions during the telephone call.

Confirm what you hear by asking questions that verify the information. Summarizing the confirmation will also help you verify additional information.

Create a comfortable feeling between you and the other party by asking questions in a pleasant manner. Avoid tension and edginess.

THE CONCLUSION

In the *conclusion* stage of a telephone call, the caller and receiver come to an understanding of the action to be taken by each of them. Then they say good-bye.

Understanding the Action to Be Taken If you are the one who is going to take action, verify what you are going to do or what will happen.

"I'll see that Ms. Schmidt gets your message as soon as she returns."

"Your order will be processed and you should receive the merchandise within ten business days."

"I will check on the status of your claim and get back to you within a day."

If you are unsure of anything that has been agreed upon during the call, confirm your information by asking closed questions.

"Will you be out of the office this afternoon?"

"Do you wish to order the office supplies at this time?"

"Is the policy issued in both you and your husband's name?"

If a lot of information has been exchanged during the call, it is helpful to summarize what has been said. This brings closure to the call and reviews the call and the action needed.

Summarizing a phone call can help avoid miscommunications later.

Closing the Telephone Call Once the two parties understand the action to be taken, they can end the call. Sometimes you must take the initiative to end a call if the other party continues to talk after the business has been conducted. You can do this courteously by saying a statement such as:

> "I appreciate your calling, Mr. Chin."

> "It was nice to speak with you today, Jim. Thanks for calling and updating me on the status of the revision."

Statements like these show interest in the other party and also communicate that you are ready to end the call.

You should always end the call by saying "good-bye" in a pleasant tone of voice. Avoid colloquial expressions (such as "talk to you later," "bye-bye," "see yah") that do not project a professional image.

End the phone call pleasantly and professionally, avoiding colloquial expressions and slang.

After you say good-bye, allow the other party to hang up first. This ensures that you do not cut the other person off too quickly. Then place the receiver gently on its cradle or press the appropriate button to terminate the call.

Summary

1. As technology advances, the telephone continues to be an important communication tool.

2. Learning how to refine your telephone skills can improve communication and goodwill in business.

3. Communication is the process of exchanging ideas and messages either verbally or nonverbally. Communication consists of four major parts: speaking, reading, writing, and listening—with listening being one of the most important.

4. Communicating on the telephone differs from communicating face-to-face: you cannot see the other person or party.

5. When you speak on the telephone, you cannot use your appearance, posture, eye contact, and gestures to help convey your message. Your voice must do the job.

6. Vary the pitch of your voice in order to make it interesting and pleasant to hear.

7. You must learn to read and interpret telephone messages successfully.

8. Listening involves four related steps: sensing, interpreting, evaluating, and responding.

9. When you use the telephone to communicate, you must practice active listening. Active listening means that you hear words and thoughts and need to respond to them.

10. When you pick up the telephone receiver, be ready to listen.

11. To deal with the roadblocks of distractions, interruptions, and disconnected calls when using the telephone, prepare for and know how to manage them.

12. Whenever you are using the telephone, keep in mind that *courtesy* and *professionalism* are the bench marks of positive telephone skills.

13. Whether you are making or answering a call, the first few seconds of the call are very important.

14. If it is necessary to put the caller on "hold," periodically ask the caller if he or she wishes to continue "holding" or to leave a message.

15. Establish the convenience of the call, particularly if it is an international call or a long-distance call involving different time zones.

16. Ask questions to obtain information you need in order to answer the other party's request or to clarify a response to your needs.

17. In the conclusion stage of a telephone call, the caller and receiver come to an understanding of the action to be taken by each of them and then say good-bye.

Reinforcement Application 1

Listening For Positive Communication

Directions: Select a partner to work with you on this speaking and listening activity. Designate one person as Partner A and the other as Partner B. Partner A should read the following statement to Partner B. Partner B should be able to hear but not see Partner A, and should be prepared to take notes. This activity is to simulate a telephone conversation between two people.

Statement: Hello, this is Courtney Eastman, Administrator of Customer Services. Please make your cashiers aware of a major problem McKenney Foods has been having with bad checks. On Thursday, June 1, a customer successfully passed a bad check in the amount of $178.35 at the North Baldwin store. The customer was using the name June Rostberg, spelled R-O-S-T-B-E-R-G. On Saturday, June 3, another bad check for $91.21 was passed at the Cornish store by a person using the name of Jan Roastberg, spelled R-O-A-S-T-B-E-R-G. On the following Tuesday, June 6, a person using the name of Jane Roseburg (R-O-S-E-B-U-R-G) passed another bad check for $158.10, again at the Cornish store. In all cases, the customer showed a form of identification that the cashier accepted. Please emphasize to your cashiers that only proper identification (driver's license or McKenney Foods check-cashing ID card) is acceptable and should be checked carefully. Thank you for your prompt attention to this matter.

Partner B should now answer the following questions:

1. Who was the caller?

   _____

2. How many bad checks were passed?

   _____

3. What were the names used by the customer?

   _____

4. What identification should the cashiers accept from customers wanting to pay by check?

   _____

   _____

   _____

5. What qualities of Partner A's voice helped you listen to and understand this statement?

_____

_____

6. What could Partner A have done to improve voice tone and speaking techniques?

_____

_____

7. What could you have done to improve your listening skill?

_____

_____

Case Study 1

The Interrupting Manager

Directions: Analyze the situation described below and then answer the questions that follow.

Kelley is the administrative assistant to three managers in the graphics art department of a large printing and desktop publishing firm. A major problem has been occurring: numerous thoughtless interruptions are occurring when people are using the telephone, due mainly to the staff's many pending deadlines. At a recent staff meeting, the situation was discussed, and everyone agreed to make an effort to be more courteous to people who are on the telephone.

Two of Kelley's managers have been very conscientious about not interrupting. This improvement has definitely made her work easier. However, the third manager has made no attempt to improve his interruptions. He walks up to Kelley's desk at will and starts to give her directions about a task while she is on the phone. He has a loud voice, which makes it difficult for Kelley to hear the person on the other end of the phone. Kelley has been forced to ask customers to hold at least three times in the last two days in order to listen to the demands of her uncooperative manager.

This situation is very embarrassing. In fact, one potential customer became very upset and hung up after holding for several minutes, even though Kelley returned to speaking to the potential customer approximately every twenty seconds.

1. How is Kelley trying to handle the problem of her managers' interruptions?

_____

_____

_____

_____

2. Do you think the fact that the third manager is one of her bosses is affecting Kelley's handling of the situation? Why or why not?

_____

_____

_____

_____

3. What steps can Kelley take to try to change the third manager's behavior?

_____

_____

_____

_____

4. How do the four major components of communication (speaking, reading, writing, and listening) affect the situation with which Kelley is faced?

_____

_____

_____

_____

CHAPTER

Processing Incoming Calls

OBJECTIVES

Chapter 2 will help you:

1. Answer the telephone in a professional manner.

2. Screen calls positively and efficiently.

3. Place calls on hold professionally and efficiently.

4. Transfer calls in a timely, professional, and efficient manner.

5. Record accurate messages that are received directly or recorded on telephone-answering equipment.

*Y*our telephone is ringing while you are on another call. You have been wait-ing for the incoming call and must act immediately on it.

This situation is repeated thousands of times daily in the business world. Mismanaging an incoming call can cause you to lose business or goodwill or both. Potential customers often take their business to another company when a telephone is not answered quickly or professionally.

PREPARING FOR INCOMING CALLS

The most important rule to pre-pare for incoming calls is, *Be pre-pared!* Arrange your work area to include the necessary materials for receiving incoming calls. Place your telephone in a convenient location. For example, if you are right-handed, place the telephone on the left side of the desk, so you can use your right hand to take messages. Do the reverse if you are left-handed. If you answer numer-ous calls, a telephone headset may be more convenient because it will free both of your hands.

Figure 2-1

Messages must be taken frequently. Have pens and message forms readily available. Also, place a clock within sight for immediate reference. Keep the telephone directories and lists of frequently used phone num-bers, extensions, e-mail addresses, and fax numbers readily available. If this information is stored on your computer, have a printed copy available in case of power outages or computer failure.

Figure 2-2　An answering machine can answer incoming calls in your absence. Be sure to follow up all messages in a timely fashion.

When you need to be away from your desk, make arrangements to have your incoming calls answered. An ***answering machine*** can answer calls in your absence. (See Figure 2-2.) This machine records callers' messages for you. Another option is to arrange for a person to answer your phone. On some telephone systems you can automatically route incoming calls to another person's line. Then, when you return to your desk, you can cancel this routing and again receive calls on your phone.

Be prepared for incoming calls. Have your tele-phone, message forms, pens, tele-phone directories, and other references readily available.

Even when you are away from your desk, have a method in place for answer-ing your incoming calls.

Some businesses use equipment that automatically answers phones that are not answered by an employee. Sometimes this equipment is used only when the business is closed. For example, a recording may ask the caller to phone back during business hours. More often, however, the answering equipment records incoming messages. If you use equipment that records messages, remember to always play back and follow up your messages.

Voice mail is an automated system used to take incoming messages. Businesses, as well as individuals, usually subscribe to voice mail through a telephone service or company. When the system receives a call, it instructs the caller how to record a message. Voice mail is discussed in greater detail in Chapter 5.

If voice mail is overused or if the person or business called does not follow up on messages, callers can become frustrated. If used properly, however, voice mail can save time and the potential loss of a customer or an important call.

ANSWERING THE TELEPHONE

When you answer the telephone, create a sense of being comfortable in speaking with the caller, and be pleasant. This will help you during the call and when concluding it.

THE ROBOT RECEPTIONIST

"Thank you for calling XYZ Company. If you are calling from a touch-tone telephone, please press 1 to place an order, press 2 to. . . ." You hear such messages quite often today—the voice of a machine known as an *automated attendant*. In other words, it is a robot receptionist. A robot receptionist is desirable when:

- Human receptionists are scarce and/or expensive.

- The receptionist has a break or is busy greeting visitors.

- Human operators need time to handle the calls that generate sales rather than merely transmitting routine information.

An effective automated attendant system increases the capacity to handle incoming calls.

ANSWERING AND MANAGING INCOMING CALLS

Keep these points in mind to help you manage incoming calls.

- **Answer your telephone immediately, preferably no later than the second ring.** This shows that you are efficient and paying attention. Callers whose calls are unanswered after repeated rings may become unhappy and frustrated.

- **Identify yourself properly in a friendly and professional manner.** This will begin the conversation pleasantly and positively.

  "Good morning, Dr. Santos' office. How may I help you?"

- **Use the caller's name if you know it.** When you use the caller's name during the call, it affirms a sense of warmth and personal interest.

  "Thank you for calling, Joyce. I will be sure that Dr. Kautz receives your message."

- **Obtain as much information as you can from the caller to help you process the call.** Practice good questioning techniques and speak clearly. Obtain as much information as possible from the callers to reduce the need to transfer calls. For example, say, "I will be glad to give Mrs. Chin your message. May I have your name, address, and telephone number, please." (See "Questioning Over the Telephone" on page 00.)

- **Do not interrupt the caller. Write one or two words on your message form that will remind you to focus on a point.** Ask your questions or make your comments when the caller stops talking.

- **Give accurate information.** If any information is unclear or you have insufficient answers to the caller's questions, say that you need the necessary information. Avoid using vague phrases, such as "I really am not sure" or "It may be that." Such phrases can convey a lack of confidence in what you are discussing.

IDENTIFYING YOURSELF

First impressions count. When identifying yourself on the telephone, your tone of voice sends an immediate and lasting message. A pleasant and cheerful "Good afternoon, Dearborn Enterprises," as opposed to a curt "Dearborn Enterprises, hold," sets the scene for a positive telephone call.

You never get a second chance to make a good first impression.

IDENTIFYING YOURSELF ON THE TELEPHONE

Follow these steps to ensure that you properly identify yourself on the telephone.

1. **Identify yourself courteously.**

   "Customer Service, Miss Rivers. May I help you?"

   "Dr. Hatch's office; this is Julie. How may I help you?"

2. **Use positive phrases when identifying yourself.**

   "Good morning, Neilson Enterprises."

   "Cornish Bank and Trust Company; this is June."

3. **Generate enthusiasm as you answer and identify yourself.** This will create a pleasant atmosphere for the entire call.

4. **Smile when you answer a telephone call.** Smiling throughout the call loosens your vocal chords, making you feel more relaxed.

The wording of a professional and courteous identification depends on your organization and your role in it. You may be answering the telephone for one of many departments, for another person, or for yourself.

ACTIVITY 10: Identify Yourself When Answering the Telephone

The purpose of this activity is to practice identifying yourself properly when you answer the telephone. Read each description and write an appropriate identification to use for incoming calls on the answer rules. Remember that an accurate identification when answering a telephone can reduce the need to repeat information—thereby helping to ensure a positive conversation.

1. Lisa Boardman is an administrative assistant answering the telephone for her manager, Elaine Hopkins.

   _____

   _____

   _____

   _____

2. Alan Wadsworth is a receptionist at the main switchboard of Barrens, Noble, and Quinn law firm.

_____

_____

_____

_____

3. Jack Vachenko is a clerk in Shipping and Receiving at the Portland, Maine, branch of Jordanski's Department Store.

_____

_____

_____

_____

4. Arlene Blair from the Marketing Department of The L. R. Green Company is answering the telephone of her coworker, Jean Sturgeon.

_____

_____

_____

_____

5. Nicholas Stacey is a sales associate in the Art Department of the Warwick Craft Store.

_____

_____

_____

_____

SCREENING CALLS

Learning to *screen* calls positively takes practice. Screening calls also involves applying sound judgment. After you identify yourself, give the caller an opportunity to identify himself or herself and to tell you the purpose of the call.

When you answer the telephone at a switchboard or on behalf of your manager, you must often screen calls. You may need to determine whether or not to forward calls to the desired party. You also may need to know how your manager wishes you to handle unwanted calls and callers who refuse to identify themselves. In addition, you should know when it is necessary to interrupt your manager and how to give information to callers without revealing too many details.

Screening an Unwanted Caller When your manager does not wish to be interrupted, you are on alert to screen calls carefully. In the following situation, Allayne Hutton is working on a report she must complete by 3 p.m. She has told her assistant, Merrillyn Stanley, not to interrupt her unless Marie Orsini calls. Merrillyn screens the first of Ms. Hutton's calls effectively, as follows.

Merrillyn:	"Ms. Hutton's office, Mrs. Stanley speaking."
Mr. Lord:	"This is Larry Lord from Lord Real Estate. May I speak to Ms. Hutton, please?"
Merrillyn:	"I'm sorry, Mr. Lord, Ms. Hutton is not available at the moment. May I have her call you?"
Mr. Lord:	"Yes, please. My number is 555-3221."
Merrillyn:	"Thank you, Mr. Lord. I'll give Ms. Hutton your number. That's 555-3221."
Mr. Lord:	"Yes, thank you. Good-bye."
Merrillyn:	"Good-bye."

Merrillyn was professional and diplomatic with Mr. Lord. She said nothing to reveal that Ms. Hutton was in the office but did not want to speak to him. Shortly after this call, Marie Orsini called, and Merrillyn transferred the call to Ms. Hutton immediately.

Screening an Unidentified Caller When a caller refuses to identify himself or herself, screen the call carefully, as in this example:

Merrillyn:	"Ms. Hutton's office, Mrs. Stanley speaking."
Caller:	"May I speak with Ms. Hutton?"
Merrillyn:	"May I ask who is calling?"
Caller:	"Just connect me to Ms. Hutton. She knows me."
Merrillyn:	"I'm sorry, but Ms. Hutton is not available at the moment. Would you like to leave a message?"
Caller:	"Uh, no. I'll call back later. Bye."
Merrillyn:	"Good-bye."

Merrillyn was courteous. She gave the caller the opportunity to identify himself or herself and to leave a message. What happens if the caller telephones again later in the day when Ms. Hutton is available? Merrillyn knows that Ms. Hutton will not take any calls unless she knows who is calling.

Merrillyn:	"Ms. Hutton's office, Mrs. Stanley speaking."
Caller:	"Hello, may I speak with Ms. Hutton?"
Merrillyn:	"May I ask who is calling?"
Caller:	"That's OK; just put me through to Ms. Hutton. I'm a personal friend of hers."
Merrillyn:	"I'm sorry, but I cannot put a call through to Ms. Hutton without knowing who is calling."
Caller:	"Oh, all right. This is Robert Rubin from Tri-County Sports."
Merrillyn:	"Thank you, Mr. Rubin. I'll see if Ms. Hutton is available."

Merrillyn was courteous but firm in insisting that the caller identify himself. She can now inform Ms. Hutton that Mr. Rubin is on the line. If Ms. Hutton does not wish to take the call, Merrillyn has left herself the option of telling Mr. Rubin that Ms. Hutton is not available to speak with him at this time.

Handling Interruptions Sometimes a caller will not accept the fact that your manager is unavailable. Apply firm yet professional judgment. If the call is an emergency, interrupt or locate your manager immediately, explaining that you have an emergency call.

If you do not know the purpose of the call but the caller is insistent, you can ask the caller to hold while you check to see if your manager is available. If your manager is not in the office, ask the caller if you or someone else might be able to help.

Know how your manager wishes you to manage specific calls; for example, calls from family members, personal friends, and designated employees and clients.

Using Discretion Wisely Being *discreet* means that you are careful not to reveal any inappropriate information. In the hypothetical situation of Ms. Hutton and her assistant, Merrillyn Stanley, one morning Ms. Hutton was late for work. She was detained because of an early morning meeting out of the office and heavy traffic on the freeway leading to the office. At 9:49, more than 45 minutes after she should have been in the office, Ms. Hutton received a call from her manager, Ben McKenney.

Merrillyn:	"Good morning, Ms. Hutton's office. Mrs. Stanley speaking."
Mr. McKenney:	"Hello, Merrillyn. This is Ben McKenney. Is Allayne there?"
Merrillyn:	"I'm sorry, Mr. McKenney, but Ms. Hutton is not available at the moment. May I have her call you?"
Mr. McKenney:	"Sure."

Merrillyn:	"I'll have her call you as soon as possible."	
Mr. McKenney:	"Thanks, Merrillyn. Good-bye."	
Merrillyn:	"Good-bye."	

Merrillyn was careful not to reveal any inappropriate information to Mr. McKenney. She did not say that Ms. Hutton was late; she simply said Ms. Hutton was not available.

The phrase "not available" safely covers a wide variety of situations in which the person called cannot come to the phone. Perhaps the person left early because of a personal matter, is in the restroom, or is meeting with an important client.

ACTIVITY 11: Screening Calls

The purpose of this activity is to help you decide what to do when you screen a telephone call. Read each situation and determine whether the call should be forwarded to the desired party. If it should be forwarded, place a check mark in the Yes column. If it should not be forwarded, place a check mark in the No column. Be prepared to explain the reason for your answer.

	Yes	No
1. A woman, who refuses to identify herself or state her business, calls and wants to speak to Mr. Ridlonsky immediately.	_____	_____
2. Mr. Ridlonsky, who had to do some personal errands, is late getting back from lunch. An important client calls and asks to speak with him.	_____	_____
3. Mr. Ridlonsky is attending an important meeting in Ms. Qantel's office. His wife calls and tells you that she must speak to him because of a family emergency.	_____	_____
4. Mr. Ridlonsky asks you to hold all of his calls for an hour. A client calls and asks to speak to him.	_____	_____
5. Mr. Ridlonsky is on the telephone with a client when his manager, Mr. Dean, calls on another line and asks to speak with him.	_____	_____

SAMPLE RESPONSES FOR INCOMING CALLS

- **When the person called is in:**

  "Yes, just a moment and I will connect you."

- **When the person called is on another line:**

  "She's talking on another line. Would you care to hold, or may I have her call you?"

- **When the person called is not in:**

  "Mr. Miliker will not be in today. Can someone else help you, or would you like to leave a message?"

  "Mr. Miliker will be out of town until next week. May I give him a message?"

  "Dr. Lupie is taking calls for Dr. Markson. May I give you that number?"

  "The department is closed for the day. Business hours are from 8 to 4:30. Would you care to call tomorrow?"

  "Ms. Scott is not available right now. Could someone else help you?"

  "I'm sorry, she is not in the office right now. Would you care to leave a message?"

  "He is away from his desk. May I ask him to call you?"

- **When screening a call:**

  "Will Mr. Lopez know what your call is about?"

  "May I tell her what the call is about?"

  "May I say who is calling, please?"

  "Just a moment and I will try to locate him for you. (*pause*) I'm sorry, he is not available. Could someone else help you?"

- **When transferring a call:**

  "That department is located in another building. Just a moment and I will transfer your call. The number is 555-8899 if you wish to call them in the future."

  "Mr. Nathan is in charge of that department, and I am sure he can help you. Just a moment and I will transfer your call. In case we are disconnected, his extension is 445."

  "Our Marketing Department can answer your question. Just a moment and I will have your call transferred."

Put a caller on hold only after you have allowed him or her to speak.

PLACING CALLERS ON HOLD

Sometimes it is necessary to place callers on *hold* so you can get information, speak to another person, or answer another call. Most telephones have a specific procedure for placing callers on hold. Become familiar with the procedure for your telephone so you do not accidentally cut off callers.

The act of putting someone on hold is not a mechanical operation. You must be both courteous and professional in the process. Never put a caller on hold before allowing him or her to speak. Wait until it is your turn to speak and then politely ask the caller to hold. See the following examples:

"One moment, please. Let me see if Ms. Edgerly is available."

"Please hold. Someone will be right with you."

"Would you mind holding for a moment, please. Another line is ringing."

Being placed on hold is not a particularly pleasant experience. This is true even when the telephone system plays soft music or messages. When you return to the caller, express appreciation for waiting. You might say something like:

"Thank you for holding, Mr. Martinez. I have your report in front of me now."

"Thank you for holding, Mary. Mr. Wadsworth's line is still busy. Would you like to continue to hold, or would you prefer to leave a message?"

Both examples show that you are concerned about and interested in the caller's needs. The caller should not feel neglected or forgotten. Most people wait patiently on hold for approximately 15 to 30 seconds.

When receiving multiple calls at the same time, keep a list of each so that you can handle all of them efficiently.

Ideally, phone calls would be received one at a time. In reality, many calls are received at the same time. Answer the lines one at a time in the order in which they are received. You might need to place one or more of the calls on hold so that you can complete or transfer others. Before placing calls on hold, make a list of each call so that you can handle all of them efficiently. Beside each extension number, list the caller's name and a brief summary of the purpose of the call. (Transferring calls is explained later in this chapter.)

COMMON-SENSE RULES FOR PUTTING A CALLER ON HOLD OR TRANSFERRING A CALL

- Let the caller know what you are doing and why.

- If a caller was on hold, be sure to express appreciation when you return to the call. "Thank you for waiting" tells the caller you are ready to resume the conversation.

- If the caller has been on hold for more than 30 seconds, check periodically to see if he or she wishes to keep waiting.

- If the call is long-distance, ask the caller for permission to put the call on hold or transfer it. Give the caller a choice.

- When transferring a call, explain briefly to the person why and to whom you are transferring the call. Let the caller know when you begin the transfer.

ACTIVITY 12: Placing Calls On and Removing Them From Hold

The purpose of this activity is to give you insight into the proper procedure for placing callers on hold and removing them from hold. Read the following examples of unprofessional telephone conversations that may occur in an office. Then, write a more positive response for each example that would make the caller feel he or she is being treated courteously and professionally.

1. **Recipient:** "Schmidt and Schroeder. Hold on, please."

   _____

   _____

   _____

   _____

2. **Recipient returning to caller placed on hold:** "Hello? Are you still there?"

   _____

   _____

   _____

   _____

3. **Caller:** "This is Brandy Stanleywood. May I speak—"
   Recipient: "Would you hold, please?"

   _____

   _____

   _____

   _____

4. **Recipient:** "Burkowski's. Hold on, I have another call."

_____

_____

_____

_____

5. **Recipient:** "Kezar Falls Pizza Shop. We're busy; can you call back in 10 minutes? I'm on another line."

_____

_____

_____

_____

TRANSFERRING A CALL

You may receive calls that another department or person is better equipped to handle. In such instances, it may be necessary to *transfer* the call. Transferring calls is commonplace in business. However, you must follow several important steps when transferring calls.

In order to transfer calls efficiently, you should know and understand the function of each department within your company. Keep a company directory handy so that you can look up the correct extension numbers before transferring a call.

When you are unsure who should handle a call, place the caller on hold and ask a coworker or manager for guidance. In some businesses you can transfer the caller back to the switchboard so that the operator can route the call to the right person or department. If your company does not have a switchboard, be sure to establish a procedure for transferring calls.

Before you transfer a call, tell the caller the person or department to whom you are transferring the call and the correct telephone number or extension.

> "Mrs. Diabo, I am transferring you to Customer Service. That number is 555-4001 in case you need it for future reference."

Most phone systems allow you to speak privately to the person receiving the transferred call. In this case, summarize the caller's business so that the caller does not have to repeat the story.

> "Elizabeth, I am transferring a call from Mrs. Diabo. She is having a problem with her Create It software."

When transferring calls, dial the extension number carefully. Avoid the need for another department or person to also transfer the call.

After you have summarized the caller's business, complete the transfer. Usually you must press a special button to place the call on the recipient's phone. Then, gently replace your handset on its cradle to disconnect your phone from the call.

Become thoroughly familiar with your telephone system so you can transfer calls efficiently. Always give the caller the number to which you are transferring the call in case you accidentally disconnect the call. Remember, you can handle only one call at a time; place other new calls on hold so you can make the transfer carefully.

ACTIVITY 13: Analyzing Incoming Calls

The purpose of this activity is to practice analyzing and improving parts of telephone conversations. Read each statement below and determine if it is acceptable. If it is, place a check mark in the Yes column. If it is not, place a check mark in the No column; then write a brief response as to why it is unacceptable. Be prepared to explain why you made your choice.

	Yes	No

1. "Maureen's not here right now. What's the message?"

   _____

   _____

   _____

2. "Hello. No, this is not Cornwall Hardware."

   _____

   _____

   _____

3. "Hold on, please; I'll transfer you. If we get disconnected, his extension is 5516."

   _____

   _____

   _____

4. "We don't deal with that item. Call the frame department."

   _____

   _____

   _____

5. "Good afternoon, this is Courtney's Bridal Shop. May I help you?"

_____ _____

_____

_____

_____

6. "Mrs. Hodgkins is at lunch and is 15 minutes overdue."

_____ _____

_____

_____

_____

RECORDING CALLS

Logging is the process of keeping track of calls. For example, salespeople keep close track of their calls so they will know when to call again or follow up. Various telephone systems allow for a variety of ways to keep track of calls. Logging may be done on a computer, or it may be done by listing incoming calls on a manual log slip. (See Figures 2-3 and 2-4.)

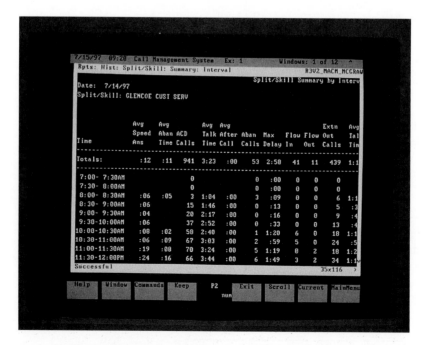

Figure 2-3   An electronic call log.

```
Telephone Call Received: ___February 4___  19 __—__

Name of Client: __Nancy Farber__

Time Called: __9:55 a.m.__  Time Ended: __10:10 a.m.__

Called Lawyer: __Susan Eigen__

In Re: __Divorce Case 4492__
```

Figure 2-4   A manual call log.

TAKING MESSAGES

With today's technology a variety of options are available for taking messages. The traditional way of taking messages on paper will always be available. Spoken messages are becoming very common. Spoken messages can be left on answering machines or on voice mail. You may be responsible for scanning and taking messages left on your manager's answering machine or voice mail. Regardless of the method, relaying messages requires clear communication.

When the person called is unavailable, ask the caller if he or she would like to leave a message with you or on the person's voice mail, if voice mail is available. If you are taking a message, listen carefully and ask questions if you do not understand something. Record the information accurately. As you listen, try to detect the tone of the caller's voice. Read numbers back to the caller in pairs to make sure you have recorded them correctly. If necessary, verify data and the spelling of names.

Most companies use message forms to record phone calls (see Figure 2-5). A complete telephone message includes the following:

- Name of the person being called.
- Caller's name.
- Caller's organization.
- Caller's telephone and extension number, with area code if the caller's number is outside the area code of the business.
- Message.
- Date and time of the call.
- Name or initials of the person taking the message.

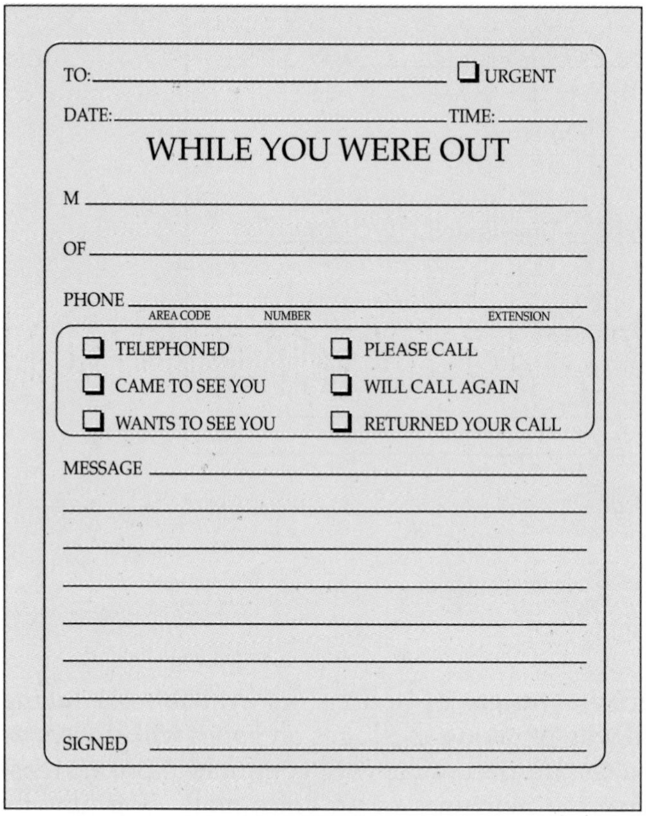

TO: ________ ❑ URGENT

DATE: ________ TIME: ________

WHILE YOU WERE OUT

M ________

OF ________

PHONE ________
AREA CODE NUMBER EXTENSION

❑ TELEPHONED ❑ PLEASE CALL
❑ CAME TO SEE YOU ❑ WILL CALL AGAIN
❑ WANTS TO SEE YOU ❑ RETURNED YOUR CALL

MESSAGE ________

SIGNED ________

Figure 2-5 A telephone message form.

You may also include the priority (e.g., urgent) of the call. Determine this from the nature of the message and the caller's tone. Also, indicate whether the caller will call again, if he or she returned a call, or other similar information.

Some phones can store and dial frequently used numbers; this is sometimes called speed dialing. If your manager does not have this feature or has not stored the caller's number, request the caller's number during the call.

A caller might say that the manager has the phone number when you ask for it. Ask again by saying something like "May I please have it to write down on the message so that Mr. Perkins won't have to look it up?"

If a caller identifies himself or herself but leaves no message or number, do not insist on one. Write all information available on the message and note "Will call again" on the message form.

Telephone tag can be frustrating. To avoid it, note on messages the suggested times for returning calls.

Try to avoid ***telephone tag***; that is, the process in which two parties return calls to each other but never make contact with one another. Tell the caller the best time to call again, or ask the caller for a good time to return the call.

Once the message form is complete, promptly deliver it to the recipient. Most message forms are printed on colored paper in order to be seen easily. Nonetheless, place the message in a location where it will be readily noticed. Prop it on the telephone or in another conspicuous spot. Never put telephone messages in places where they may be covered under other material. Ask your manager to designate a specific area in which to leave his or her messages.

ACTIVITY 14: Incomplete Messages

The purpose of this activity is to emphasize the importance of taking a complete telephone message. For each item below, transfer the information to the message forms provided on page 46. After you have completed each message form, you will notice that important information is missing!

1. Message for Jean Bragman
   Sarah Simmonds of Educational Visuals called.
   Please call her.
   February 23, 10:45 a.m.
   JM

2. G. W. Maxwell called.
   (601) 555-8734
   Please call him.
   April 17, 1:45 p.m.

3. Message for Kelly Cummings
   Steve O'Conner from the Irish International Council called.
   (212) 555-3500
   Please call him about his passport.
   Jack

4. Message for Maureen Parker
   Mike Pankowitz of the Portland Wordsmiths Book Store
   He will call back tomorrow.
   Sally

Call 1

Here is a Message for You

To _____

_____

of _____

Phone No. _____ Ext. _____

☐ Telephoned   ☐ Will Call Again
☐ Returned Your Call   ☐ Came To See You
☐ Please Phone   ☐ Wants To See You

_____
_____
_____
_____

| Taken By | Date | Time |

Call 2

Here is a Message for You

To _____

_____

of _____

Phone No. _____ Ext. _____

☐ Telephoned   ☐ Will Call Again
☐ Returned Your Call   ☐ Came To See You
☐ Please Phone   ☐ Wants To See You

_____
_____
_____
_____

| Taken By | Date | Time |

Call 3

Here is a Message for You

To _____

_____

of _____

Phone No. _____ Ext. _____

☐ Telephoned   ☐ Will Call Again
☐ Returned Your Call   ☐ Came To See You
☐ Please Phone   ☐ Wants To See You

_____
_____
_____
_____

| Taken By | Date | Time |

Call 4

Here is a Message for You

To _____

_____

of _____

Phone No. _____ Ext. _____

☐ Telephoned   ☐ Will Call Again
☐ Returned Your Call   ☐ Came To See You
☐ Please Phone   ☐ Wants To See You

_____
_____
_____
_____

| Taken By | Date | Time |

The purpose of this activity is to practice recording complete messages based on information provided. For each call below, record a complete message, using the forms provided on page 48.

1. On Friday, June 1, at 10:30 a.m. Carolyn Hodges of the Bar Harbor Hotel called, asking to speak to Sharon Miller. She wants to discuss the retirement party Ms. Miller is planning. Ms. Hodges can be reached at 555-3297 between 2 and 3 p.m. today.

2. You took a message for Katie Sargent at 12:19 on Wednesday, November 17, from a person identifying herself only as Suzanne. She said Katie would know who she was. She needs to speak to Katie as soon as possible. Katie should call her before 3:45 at 212-555-1208.

3. Peter Crosson received a call from Jessica Sefcik of the Map Center at 4:30 p.m. on Friday, June 1. Mr. Crosson had already left for the weekend when the call was received. Ms. Sefcik wants Peter to know she mailed the information he requested by express mail and he should receive it on Monday. If he has questions, he can call her on Monday at 301-555-2334.

4. Marilyn Williams of the Island Development Corporation called on July 3 at 10 a.m., asking to speak to Matthew Lukas. She wants him to call her on July 8 after 11 a.m. at 555-3400.

Call 1

| TO: | | ☐ URGENT |
| DATE: | | TIME: |

WHILE YOU WERE OUT

M _____

OF _____

PHONE _____
AREA CODE   NUMBER   EXTENSION

☐ TELEPHONED   ☐ PLEASE CALL
☐ CAME TO SEE YOU   ☐ WILL CALL AGAIN
☐ WANTS TO SEE YOU   ☐ RETURNED YOUR CALL

MESSAGE _____
_____
_____
_____
_____
_____

SIGNED _____

Call 2

| TO: | | ☐ URGENT |
| DATE: | | TIME: |

WHILE YOU WERE OUT

M _____

OF _____

PHONE _____
AREA CODE   NUMBER   EXTENSION

☐ TELEPHONED   ☐ PLEASE CALL
☐ CAME TO SEE YOU   ☐ WILL CALL AGAIN
☐ WANTS TO SEE YOU   ☐ RETURNED YOUR CALL

MESSAGE _____
_____
_____
_____
_____
_____

SIGNED _____

Call 3

| TO: | | ☐ URGENT |
| DATE: | | TIME: |

WHILE YOU WERE OUT

M _____

OF _____

PHONE _____
AREA CODE   NUMBER   EXTENSION

☐ TELEPHONED   ☐ PLEASE CALL
☐ CAME TO SEE YOU   ☐ WILL CALL AGAIN
☐ WANTS TO SEE YOU   ☐ RETURNED YOUR CALL

MESSAGE _____
_____
_____
_____
_____
_____

SIGNED _____

Call 4

| TO: | | ☐ URGENT |
| DATE: | | TIME: |

WHILE YOU WERE OUT

M _____

OF _____

PHONE _____
AREA CODE   NUMBER   EXTENSION

☐ TELEPHONED   ☐ PLEASE CALL
☐ CAME TO SEE YOU   ☐ WILL CALL AGAIN
☐ WANTS TO SEE YOU   ☐ RETURNED YOUR CALL

MESSAGE _____
_____
_____
_____
_____
_____

SIGNED _____

Summary

1. The most important rule to prepare for incoming calls is, *Be prepared*.

2. Arrange your work area so that the materials necessary to receive incoming calls are available.

3. Voice mail is an automated system used to take incoming messages. If it is overused or if the recipient of the call does not follow up on messages, callers may become frustrated.

4. When you need to be away from your desk, make arrangements to have your incoming calls answered.

5. Some businesses use equipment that automatically answers phones that are not answered by an employee.

6. If the telephone equipment you use records messages, remember to always play back and follow up your messages.

7. When you answer the telephone, create a sense of being comfortable in speaking with the caller, and be pleasant.

8. When identifying yourself on the telephone, be aware that your tone of voice sends an immediate and lasting message.

9. The wording of a professional and courteous identification depends on your organization and your role within it.

10. Learning to screen calls positively takes practice. Screening calls also involves applying sound judgment.

11. Know when it is necessary to interrupt your manager.

12. Being discreet means that you are careful not to reveal any inappropriate information or too many details.

13. Most telephones have a specific procedure for placing callers on hold. Become familiar with the procedure for your telephone so you do not accidentally cut off callers.

14. Putting someone on hold is not a mechanical operation. You must be courteous and professional in the process.

15. In order to transfer calls efficiently, learn the function of each department within your company.

16. Become thoroughly familiar with your telephone system so you can transfer calls efficiently.

17. *Logging* is the process of keeping track of calls.

18. If you are taking a message, listen carefully and ask questions if you do not understand something. Record the information accurately.

19. Ask your manager to designate a specific area to leave his or her messages.

Reinforcement Application 2

Arranging a Workstation

Directions: Analyze the situation described below and then answer the questions that follow.

Grace Day is moving to a new office. Except for the telephone, which is on the left side of the desk, and a computer terminal, which is on a computer table on the right, the workstation is empty. Grace is bringing the following items with her:

a. Pen and pencil holder

b. Pad of message forms

c. Company telephone directory

d. Latest company product catalog and price lists

e. Rotary file that contains frequently used numbers

f. Extra pens and pencils

g. Pad of 8 1/2 " x 11" paper

h. Ream of 8 1/2 " x 11" white paper

i. Envelopes

j. Boxes of paper clips and staples

k. Box of blank disks

l. Copies of recent product advertisements

m. Reference materials (dictionary, atlas, thesaurus)

1. Grace is right-handed. Should she move the telephone? Why or why not?

   _____

   _____

   _____

2. Write the letters of the items you think Grace will need to use when she takes notes or messages.

   _____

3. Write the letters of the items you think Grace will need to use when she transfers a call.

   _____

4. Write the letters of the items you think Grace will need to use when giving product information to a customer.

   _____

5. Write the letters of the items you think Grace should place on top of the desk.

_____

Other comments: _____

_____

_____

Reinforcement Application 3

Screening Calls

Directions: In the space provided, indicate how you would handle each of the following situations.

1. You are answering the phone for Juliana, a coworker, who left early for a doctor's appointment. Juliana receives a call from a supplier who has a question about a recent order.

   _____

   _____

2. Your manager is in his office interviewing a job applicant and has asked not to be disturbed. The president of the company calls and asks to speak to your manager, saying it is important. This has never happened before.

   _____

   _____

   _____

3. You are managing the company switchboard, and an angry customer calls. He will not give his name or state his business. He insists on speaking to the president of the company, who is out of town.

   _____

   _____

   _____

4. Your manager is working on some routine correspondence when her brother calls.

   _____

   _____

   _____

5. Your manager has asked you to hold all of her calls except for Juanita McGregor, an important client. Ms. McGregor's business partner calls.

_____

_____

_____

Case Study 2

The Inconsiderate Representative

Directions: Analyze the situation described below and then answer the questions that follow.

Ariel Delaney has just been promoted to supervisor in the customer service department of a toy manufacturer. In her new position, she is responsible for overseeing the activities of three customer service representatives. On her second day on the job, Ariel overheard one of the representatives, Craig Albertson, making these comments and responses on the telephone:

a. (*In the middle of a call*) "Excuse me, sir. Please hold."

b. (*Answering the other line*) "Playtime, please hold."

c. (*Returning to the first call*) "Hello? Are you still there? . . . What seems to be the problem, sir? . . . Did you check the package to make sure you received five connectors?"

d. "Only four connectors? Well, there should be five. Give me your name and address, and we'll send you another one."

e. "That's ZIP Code 2 0 0 3 4." (*Ending the call*)

f. (*Returning to the second call*) "Hello? Are you still there? May I help you?"

g. "Oh, you've got the wrong department. I'll transfer you."

After she heard this, Ariel was quite upset. She thought all representatives were trained on correct telephone techniques when they were hired. It was apparent that at least one representative had missed the training.

1. For each lettered item below that corresponds to a conversation excerpt above, briefly describe Craig's error(s) in telephone technique.

a. _____

b. _____

c. _____

d. _____

e. _____

f. _____

g. _____

2. For each lettered item below that corresponds to a conversation excerpt above, rephrase Craig's portion of the conversation to be more professional and courteous.

a. _____

b. _____

c. _____

d. _____

e. _____

f. _____

g. _____

3. When Ariel schedules a training session for Craig, what aspects of answering incoming calls should be emphasized?

_____

_____

_____

Making Telephone Calls

OBJECTIVES

Chapter 3 will help you:

1. Recognize the importance of planning when making a telephone call.

2. Refine your telephone attitude when making a telephone call.

3. Use references efficiently when making a telephone call.

4. Understand the types of telephone calls and the best use of each.

5. Learn the types of services that telephone providers offer.

6. Practice telephone security and safety.

You and millions of other people use the telephone daily for many reasons. To avoid wasting time and harming the image of your business, it is important that you make positive telephone calls with efficiency. Think about your telephone skills when you make a telephone call. An awareness of your skills will help you improve them.

ASSESSMENT 2: Your Telephone Readiness

Are you ready to make a telephone call? Complete each statement below by placing a check mark under the appropriate column. Try to be as objective as possible when you assess your telephone readiness.

	Always	Usually	Sometimes
1. I am thinking positively about the telephone call I am about to make.	_____	_____	_____
2. I know why I am making this telephone call.	_____	_____	_____
3. I have all the necessary information with me before I begin the telephone call.	_____	_____	_____
4. I am scheduling my telephone call at a convenient time.	_____	_____	_____
5. I am certain that I have the correct number and have used a current telephone directory.	_____	_____	_____
6. I use directory assistance only as a last resort.	_____	_____	_____
7. I am familiar with telephone services available for my use at no charge.	_____	_____	_____
8. I use optional telephone services in a timely manner.	_____	_____	_____
9. I try to practice applicable phone security and safety at all times.	_____	_____	_____
10. I try to be aware of time used and charges concerning telephone use.	_____	_____	_____

PREPARING TO MAKE A TELEPHONE CALL

Remember to smile as you speak on the phone. This is important in positive telephone skill.

Proper attitude is crucial to making a successful and positive telephone call. Before you make a call, be mentally ready to initiate it and know the purpose of it. You might make a telephone call to:

- Provide or confirm information.

- Return a call.

- Solve a problem.

As the call progresses, anticipate possible outcomes and plan ahead on how to deal with them. Always be prepared with the necessary materials before you make the call. Have account numbers, a catalog, an electronic file, or a list of points to discuss at your fingertips.

Your manager may ask you to make a call for him or her. Understand what your manager wants you to accomplish with the call. The manager may simply want you to get the other party on the line, or he or she may want you to conduct business with the other person. Whatever the case may be, carefully plan ahead for the call.

Remember these basic steps when you make a telephone call:

1. **Identify yourself immediately and greet the person.** This starts the call on a good note.

2. **Tell the person why you are calling.** Choose your words wisely.

3. **Ask questions so that both of you understand the call, and decide the action needed.**

4. **Close the call in a friendly manner, and be sure that you and the recipient understand the outcomes that are to occur as a result of the call.**

For example, assume that you are making an airline reservation for your manager. You will need to know the following information before making the call:

- What are the dates of departure and return?

- What time does your manager want to leave and return?

- Does your manager prefer one airline over another?

- Does your manager prefer an aisle or a window seat?

- Does your manager require a special meal on the plane?

- Does your manager have a frequent-flyer membership with any of the airlines?

As you make the reservation, ask questions such as the following:

- Are the tickets refundable?

- Is the flight nonstop? If not, how many stops will the plane make? In what cities will the plane stop?

- What is the size of the plane?

- Are alternative flights available?

- Are there any restrictions on changing the flight once the ticket is purchased?

- Must the ticket be purchased within a certain period of time?

- Do the ticket prices vary, depending on the time and/or day of the flight?

In order to make a successful airline reservation, all of this information is essential. As the call continues, you might think of other questions to ask as you obtain more information. If you do not know some important information, you could cause a delay during the call or need to make several calls. It pays to be prepared before you make a call!

SCHEDULE THE CALL

You have control over when you want to make a call. Consider your own readiness and the time of day. If you call businesses who are located in different time zones, you need to call during their business hours. Refer to the time zone map in your local telephone directory to verify the time difference between your location and the recipient's. A map of area codes and time zones in North America is shown on page 148. If necessary, check the international country and city codes page in your telephone directory. In addition to the codes, some directories list the time difference from a specific time zone to other countries. (See Figure 3-1.)

International Calling Codes

	Time Difference		Time Difference		Time Difference
Algeria *213	+6	**China 86**	+13	Guatemala City 2	
American Samoa *684	-6	Beijing (Peking) 1		**Guyana 592**	+2
Argentina 54	+2	Guangzhou (Canton) 20		**Haiti 509**	0
Buenos Aires 1		Shanghai 21		Port au Prince 1	
Aruba 297	+1	**Colombia 57**	0	**Honduras* 504**	-1
Australia 61	+15	Bogota 1		**Hong Kong** 852**	+13
Melbourne 3		**Costa Rica* 506**	-1	**Hungary 36**	+6
Sydney 2		**Cyprus 357**	+7	Budapest 1	
Austria 43	+6	**Czech Republic 42**	+6	**Iceland 354**	+5
Vienna 1		Prague 2		Reykjavik 1	
Bahrain* 973	+8	**Denmark 45**	+6	**India 91**	+10½
Bangladesh 880	+11	Copenhagen 1 or 2		Bombay 22	
Belgium 32	+6	**Ecuador 593**	0	Calcutta 33	
Antwerp 3		Guayaquil 4		New Delhi 11	
Brussels 2		Quito 2		**Indonesia 62**	+12
Belize 501	-1	**Egypt 20**	+7	Jakarta 21	
Bolivia 591	+1	Alexandria 3		**Iran 98**	+8½
La Paz 2		Cairo 2		Teheran 21	
Brazil 55	+2	**El Salvador* 503**	-1	**Iraq 964**	+8
Brasilia 61		**Ethiopia 251**	+8	Baghdad 1	
Rio de Janeiro 21		Addis Ababa 1		**Ireland 353**	+5
Sao Paulo 11		**Fiji* 679**	+17	Dublin 1	
Cameroon* 237	+6	**Finland 358**	+7	**Israel 972**	+7
Chile 56	+1	Helsinki 0		Jerusalem 2	
Santiago 2	+13	**Guatemala 502**	-1	Tel Aviv 3	

Figure 3-1

You may be able to leave a message on an answering machine or voice mail, if necessary. Remember, though, that while these features are common in the United States, not all parts of the world use them.

ACTIVITY 16: Making Long-Distance Calls at the Right Time

The purpose of this activity is to help you analyze the appropriate time to make long-distance domestic and international calls.

Assume that it is 9 a.m. in your office in Boston, Massachusetts. You have several calls to make to branch offices of your company located both in the United States and overseas. Your know that the office hours at all locations are from 9 a.m. to 5 p.m. Monday through Friday.

Refer to the time zone chart in your local telephone directory. Then, write the local time next to each item below. Place a check mark by Call Now *or* Do Not Call Now *according to whether it would be appropriate to call at 9 a.m. Boston time.*

	Time	Call Now	Do Not Call Now
1. Los Angeles, California	_____	_____	_____
2. Miami, Florida	_____	_____	_____
3. Dallas, Texas	_____	_____	_____
4. Chicago, Illinois	_____	_____	_____
5. Seattle, Washington	_____	_____	_____
6. Amsterdam, The Netherlands	_____	_____	_____
7. Stockholm, Sweden	_____	_____	_____
8. Cape Town, South Africa	_____	_____	_____
9. Geneva, Switzerland	_____	_____	_____
10. London, United Kingdom	_____	_____	_____

LOCATE THE TELEPHONE NUMBER

Make sure that you have the correct telephone number before you place the call. Otherwise, you could waste time and money by searching for it or reaching the wrong person. You can locate telephone numbers by using personal directories, company directories, and local telephone directories (such as the *Yellow Pages* or *White Pages*). Business cards and some references for telephone numbers also list fax numbers and e-mail addresses.

If you cannot find a telephone number in a local, personal, or other telephone directory, call **directory assistance** for help. Be aware that many telephone companies restrict the number of times that you can use directory assistance without a charge.

Be certain that you use the telephone number, not the fax number, when making a call.

Directory assistance, or Information, can help you locate local or long-distance telephone numbers.

TELEPHONE DIRECTORIES

THE WHITE PAGES

A local telephone directory is sometimes called the *White Pages*. This directory provides an alphabetic listing of names and telephone numbers and other telephone reference information. The front pages usually contain information about area codes; billing; customer service; directory assistance; local, long-distance, and international calls; time zones; rates; emergency numbers; and other items relating to telephone use.

The next section of the telephone directory typically contains the **residence listings**, or entries, of community residents. The next section contains **business listings**, or entries, of local businesses and organizations. In some less populated or rural areas, the residence and business listings may be combined in one section.

Some local directories contain listings of local, state, and federal government offices and agencies. These listings might be incorporated into the business listing section, or they may be in a separate section of the phone book. These government listings typically are arranged by the name of the state government (such as *Maine, State of*) and then by departments or agencies. See Figure 3-2 for examples of government listings.

Figure 3-2 Residential and government office listings from a White Pages directory.

THE YELLOW PAGES

The *Yellow Pages* is a directory of listings or display ads for organizations and businesses. The listings and ads are arranged alphabetically by subject heading. Often they are cross-referenced under related subjects. The *Yellow Pages* can appear within the telephone directory, or it may be published separately. See Figure 3-3 for a sample of business listings.

Figure 3-3 Listings from a Yellow Pages directory.

Use the *Yellow Pages* when you need to locate a product or service. For example, if you need information about purchasing a new computer, look for the heading "computers." This listing will contain several businesses from which to select. If you cannot locate information on a particular topic in the *Yellow Pages*, search under related headings or subjects.

ACTIVITY 17: "Let Your Fingers Do the Walking"

The purpose of this activity is to practice locating information in the Yellow Pages. *Using the* Yellow Pages *of your local telephone directory, list the names and phone numbers of at least two suppliers for each of the following products and services.*

1. Advertising Agencies and Counselors

   _____

   _____

   _____

2. Limousine Services

   _____

   _____

   _____

3. Tire Dealers

_____

_____

_____

4. Movers

_____

_____

_____

5. Restaurants

_____

_____

_____

USING TELEPHONE DIRECTORIES

The first step in locating the telephone number of a business or residence is to know its name and its correct spelling. Residence listings are arranged alphabetically by the last name. First names appear below each last name, also in alphabetical order.

Business listings also are arranged alphabetically. If a person's name represents the company name, the entry will be under the last name (for example, *DENHAM Anne atty*). Otherwise, the company name will be listed under its first major word (for example, *Music Extravaganza The*).

RULES FOR ALPHABETIZING AND ORGANIZING BUSINESS OR RESIDENT NAMES

Study the following rules on how directory entries are alphabetized and organized.

- **A name may be listed in alternate ways.** For example, suppose you find that Neil Walter's phone number is not listed under *WALTER Neil* as you expect. The name may be listed as *NEIL Walter* (assuming you have reversed the names) or *WALTER N.* Common first names may be abbreviated; for example, *William, Robert,* and *Thomas* may be shown as *Wm, Robt,* and *Thos,* respectively.

- **An ampersand (&), hyphen (-), and apostrophe (') are overlooked in alphabetizing.** Names such as *Martin & Mason, Martin-Miller,* and *Martin's Consulting Firm* are listed in alphabetic order without considering the ampersand (&), hyphen (-), or apostrophe ('). The underlined part of the following listings was considered in alphabetizing.

Martin Kerry

Martin & Mason

Martin-Miller Jeffrey

Martin's Consulting Firm

Martin's Diner

- **An initial precedes first names that begin with that initial.** The initial *N* representing a first name would appear before the first names *Nathan* and *Nicole*. Study this example:

STEVENS A

      Annie

      E

      Emerson

      Emily

- **A name in all-capital letters appears at the beginning of its letter section.** These entries would be found at the beginning of the *W* section.

WABG Radio

WCNE TV

WSI Wallpapers

- **A number in a name is alphabetized as if it were spelled out as a word.** A number will be shown as a number in its listing (if that is the official format in the company or organization name). However, the number will be alphabetized as though it were spelled out as a word. For example:

Saw Mill Cafe

7 Seas Restaurant

Silver Spoon Inn

Soup to Nuts Lunch Stop

- **A prefix in a name is considered part of the name.** Names with prefixes are not listed separately. The underlined part in these listings shows how the entries were alphabetized.

Macadamia Nut House

MacDonald's Kitchen

Mackenzie's Market

<u>Mc</u>Donald's of Cornish

- **A common abbreviation is alphabetized as if it were spelled out.** For example, *St. George's Church* would be alphabetized as if it were spelled *Saint George's Church*. The underlined part in these listings shows how the entries were alphabetized.

<u>ST C</u>lair David

<u>SAINT G</u>eneva

<u>ST J</u>EAN Carl & Barbara

- **The word *the* at the beginning of an organization name is not considered in alphabetizing.** The company *The Musical Store*, for example, would be listed under the letter *M*. Study these examples:

Muse Barbara LISW

Music Box Retreat The

Music Junction

Musical Store The

- **A cross-reference may list common spelling variations.** At the beginning of the list of names, a cross-reference may direct you to other spellings. For example, the name *Smith* has variations like *Smythe* and *Smithe*. For example, you may see:

SMITH—See also Schmidt, Schmind, Schmitt, Smyth, Smythe

USING PERSONAL DIRECTORIES

A personal directory is your own record of frequently called numbers. Common formats are an electronic list or database on a computer, a small book with alphabetical listings, or a rotary file on your desk. Whatever format you use, be sure your personal directory is current, easy to read, and within close reach.

USING COMPANY DIRECTORIES

Many companies publish directories to make internal communication easier and more efficient. Formats include electronic lists, or databases, and hard copies in looseleaf binders. These directories may list phone numbers by department, alphabetic lists of employees, and employees' extensions. An *extension* is usually a two-, three-, or four-digit number.

USING DIRECTORIES TO MAKE INTERNATIONAL CALLS

Today it is simple to dial anywhere in the world. In fact, most international calls can be dialed direct. Most long-distance companies handle international calls. If yours does not, ask another long-distance company in your area to process your international calls. Your telephone directory may list a special number to call for information on these companies.

To make an international call, you will need to dial an international access code, a country code, a city code, and finally the local number. Most telephone directories include a list of the country codes and city codes for major foreign cities. These directories also explain how to make an international call. Dial each number carefully and slowly. Notify the international call provider if you reach an incorrect number; you should receive credit on charges for the call.

USING DIRECTORY ASSISTANCE

To access a database provided by your local telephone company, you would need the appropriate communications software, a computer, and a modem.

Directory assistance is convenient and helpful, but using it may add charges to your phone bill. First try one of these options for locating phone numbers: use your phone directory, refer to a list of frequently called numbers, or access the local *White Pages* or *Yellow Pages* database provided by your local telephone company.

When the above options are impossible, unsuccessful, or impractical, use *directory assistance*. Directory assistance provides access to many numbers. When you dial the directory assistance number, an operator will assist you with locating a number and/or an address. Usually you must give the name of the city where the business or residence you are seeking is located. Then the operator or a recording will provide the information.

Long-distance directory assistance: 1+Area Code+ 555-1212

Refer to your local directory to find the local directory assistance number. To reach directory assistance in a distant city, you need the area code of that city. Refer to the informational pages of your telephone directory for a listing of area codes for each state (often shown on a map of the United States). Once you locate the area code, dial 1 + Area Code + 555-1212 to reach directory assistance for that city. Toll-free numbers can be located by dialing 1-800-555-1212.

Toll-free number directory assistance: 1-800-555-1212

Most phone companies limit the number of times you can use directory assistance in a certain period without incurring charges. A charge is incurred for each use beyond the limit. In addition, phone companies often limit the number of items you can request per call. For example, you may be allowed to make two requests per call (such as telephone number and address) and three calls within a given period of time (usually the customer's billing period). Check with your local telephone service provider about these policies.

Keep in mind that an extra charge is usually incurred whenever an operator is involved in your call.

ACTIVITY 18: Locating Telephone Numbers

The purpose of this activity is to help you determine the correct reference for locating telephone numbers. Indicate where you would most likely find the telephone numbers for the following people or businesses. Use choices a through e for your responses.

a. Personal telephone directory

b. Company telephone directory

c. *Local* Yellow Pages

d. *Local* White Pages

e. Directory assistance

_____ 1. Your carpool members

_____ 2. A company that sells computer supplies

_____ 3. The name of your local doctor

_____ 4. A list of coworkers

_____ 5. Graham Station Restaurant in Gorham

_____ 6. The name of your closest florist

_____ 7. The Human Resources Department

_____ 8. The name of a friend whose number you lost and whose name you cannot locate in the local or your personal telephone directory

_____ 9. A car dealer

_____ 10. Polina Olanovich, a possible customer, living in Old Orchard Beach

OTHER TYPES OF OPERATOR-ASSISTED CALLS

Collect calls:
0 + Area Code +
number

Collect Calls In a **collect call** the person called agrees to pay the charges. To activate this type of call, dial 0 + Area Code + telephone number. If you hear programmed instructions, listen to and follow them carefully. If an operator answers, say you are making a collect call, then give your name and the recipient's name. The operator will dial the person's number, say who is calling, and verify whether the recipient will accept the charges for the call. If the recipient agrees, the operator will leave the line. If the recipient does not agree, the operator cannot complete the call.

Third-number
billing:
0 + Area Code +
number

Third-Number Billing **Third-number billing** bills a long-distance call to a phone besides the one you are calling to or from. To activate this type of call, dial 0 + Area Code + telephone number. You might reach an automated system. If you reach an automated system, listen to and follow the directions. If an operator comes on the line, say you wish to charge the call to a third number and give that number with area code. In some situations, the operator may verify whether the third-number party will accept the charges. If no confirmation is received, the operator cannot complete the call unless you make other billing arrangements.

Person-to-person
calls:
0 + Area Code +
number

Person-to-Person Calls A **person-to-person call** allows you to speak only with a specific person (in some cases, an extension). You will need operator assistance to make a person-to-person call. To make a person-to-person call, dial 0 + Area Code + number.

Cellular Calls Cellular, or mobile, phones in vehicles, planes, and boats can be used to make and receive telephone calls. You can usually place outgoing calls by dialing direct. However, from some places, you may need operator assistance. When you place calls from a cellular phone, you may need to use specific codes provided by the cellular phone service.

Because of their convenience, cellular phones are becoming increasingly popular. Many cellular phone providers offer competitive services and rates to their customers. Keep in mind that charges for air time can be expensive, especially at times of peak demand.

USING CELLULAR OR MOBILE PHONES

Using or holding a cellular or mobile phone while driving a vehicle (or boat) can impair your ability to focus safely on traffic. Keep these safety suggestions in mind when using a cellular phone.

- Cellular phones are safest in cars with automatic transmissions. Dialing and switching gears are not a safe mix.

- Install the phone on the dashboard of the car or elsewhere within the driver's easy reach.

- Use a hands-free phone or speaker phone.

(continued on next page)

- Learn to operate the phone without looking at it. Practice dialing while your car is stationary. In addition, use the memory feature of your phone, if there is one, to store frequently used numbers.

- If possible, dial the phone when the car is stopped for a light. If you cannot do so, dial only one or two numbers at a time, checking the traffic in between. If possible, let a passenger dial the number for you.

- Reduce your speed when driving while using the phone.

- Tell the party to whom you are speaking that you are using a car phone. This will help the person understand if you must stop talking and deal with an emergency.

- Pull over to the side of the road or into a parking lot when taking notes.

- Replace the phone securely in its cradle so that it will not dislodge.

- If you see a "Danger—blasting!" sign on the road, turn off your cellular phone. Radio waves from your phone could trigger an explosion at the blasting site.

Using an air phone is convenient, although privacy and quiet are not ensured. Some planes have phones attached to each seat; others have phones that are shared by several people. Keep these suggestions in mind when using an air phone.

If you are using a shared air phone:

- Do not stand in the aisles waiting to use a phone.

- Keep calls short so that others can use the phone.

- If you take a phone to your seat, return it as soon as possible.

- If you plan to make more than a couple of calls, try to get an aisle seat so that you do not have to climb over people.

When using any air phone:

- Keep your voice low so that you do not disturb others near you.

- Be alert for the seatbelt sign and other directions from the crew.

Conference Calls **Conference calls** permit three or more parties to communicate on a single call, which saves time and costs. Conference calls may be any combination of local or long-distance calls. They usually require operator assistance. When you arrange a conference call, provide the operator with the names and numbers of all the parties involved and a time that the call is to occur. Allow a few minutes for all the parties to be connected.

Your telephone system may enable you to complete a conference call yourself. Check first with your service provider before requesting operator assistance.

TELEPHONE SERVICES

Many telephone services are available and vary by geographic location. Some people prefer to have basic telephone services; others prefer advanced features. The fees for each service vary, and some are available at no charge.

OPTIONAL SERVICES AVAILABLE WITHOUT CHARGE

Calling Card A **calling card** is a card assigned to an individual or a telephone number. With a calling card, you can make calls from almost any location in the United States without coins and with little or no operator assistance. Calling cards are provided by most major long-distance telephone companies. Charges for calls made with a calling card appear on the monthly telephone bill.

Prepaid Phone Card A **prepaid phone card** can make the process of calling more convenient. Similar to a calling card, it allows the user to make telephone calls without coins, because the charges are paid for in advance. Usually an access code or number must be dialed to begin processing the call. Prepaid phone cards are available from many sources and in various allotments of time or dollar amounts.

Touch-Tone Service **Touch-tone service** makes the dialing process easier and quicker by allowing you to complete many "computer-assisted" calls that require you to select options using phone buttons. (These calls recognize the unique tone represented by each touch-tone button.) Push-button telephones without touch-tone service perform similarly to rotary-dial phones.

Directory Listing **Phone-number-only** service allows you to list your name and home number and just a portion or none of your address in the directory. Some customers prefer not to list their addresses for security reasons.

Two-Person Directory Listing allows two people with the same last name living at the same address to list both of their first names in the directory at no charge. For example:

MATHEWS Sebastian & Veronica

Use caution when using a calling card! Shield the phone as much as possible when inputting the card number so that people behind or beside you cannot see the numbers you are pressing. Anyone detecting these numbers can make calls that will be charged to your number.

The purpose of this activity is to help you analyze and choose appropriate operator-assisted telephone services. Assume that you want to make each of the calls below. For each call, indicate the most appropriate service from the list provided. Write the letter of your selection in the spaces provided (more than one selection may be appropriate).

    a. Direct-dial call (station-to-station)

    b. Person-to-person call

    c. Collect call

    d. Calling card call

    e. Third-number billing call

    f. Toll-free 800 number call

    g. International direct-dial call

    h. International operator-assisted call

    i. Cellular (or mobile or marine) call

    j. Conference call

_____ 1. You are driving the company car to pick up an order at a printer. On your way back to the office, you are delayed because of a major accident on your route.

_____ 2. You want to call your Uncle Emerson, who lives only a few blocks from you.

_____ 3. You are at a coin-operated phone and need to call your office. You have no change.

_____ 4. You are at the airport without your calling card and need to reach a business associate at her home. You have no change, but you know that your administrative assistant is in the office today.

_____ 5. You are traveling on business and need to speak to Elizabeth Littlejohn—and only Elizabeth!—who is handling your travel itinerary.

_____ 6. You wish to call your partner on her cellular phone.

_____ 7. Your want to phone home from a business trip (long-distance), but you have no money. You know that your mother is visiting at your home.

_____ 8. You need to speak with several business associates at the same time.

_____ 9. You want to call your manager in London, and you have his telephone number handy.

_____ 10. You want to speak to your close friend, who lives 350 miles away.

OPTIONAL SERVICES AVAILABLE FOR A MONTHLY CHARGE

The following optional services carry a monthly charge that varies with the geographic location. Your local telephone directory or telephone company can provide further information on the charges within your area.

Nondirectory Listed Number With **nondirectory listed number** service, your telephone number will not appear in the telephone directory but will be available from directory assistance.

Nonpublished Number With **nonpublished number** service, your telephone number will not appear in the telephone directory and will not be released by directory assistance.

Additional Listing With **additional listing** service, several people with the same phone number may each have a separate listing in the directory. Usually it is possible to request as many listings as desirable for an individual telephone number.

OPTIONAL CUSTOM SERVICES

Call Waiting **Call waiting** is a service that alerts you, while you are on a call, that you have an incoming call. With call waiting, you will hear a quiet beeping tone during the current call. You can then place the first call on hold in order to answer the second call; doing so ensures that you never miss a call. With a similar service, **selective call waiting**, you can temporarily cancel the call-waiting tone so that it will not interrupt the current conversation.

Call Forwarding **Call forwarding** is a service that allows you to transfer incoming calls to another number. This service is helpful if you are going to be unavailable at your usual number. Some systems provide **busy call forwarding**, which transfers incoming calls automatically when the line called is busy. **Delayed call forwarding** transfers calls automatically if the phone is not answered within a specified number of rings.

Speed Calling **Speed Calling** allows you to dial frequently called local and long-distance numbers automatically. You must use a code or series of codes that are programmed into the telephone. Instead of dialing the full number, you can dial the one- or two-digit code that you establish for the full number. Similar to speed calling, some phones *redial* the last number called when a special key is pressed or a code is entered.

Automatic Callback An **automatic callback** service, or **repeat dialing**, redials the last number called when that line is no longer busy. This service checks the line for several minutes, eliminating the need to redial repeatedly. The connection will be completed when you pick up the receiver.

Call Pickup A **call pickup** service enables an individual to pick up an incoming call on any telephone within a system (such as a company). The user must enter a code to pick up the call. Other users within the system can continue to use their phones as usual. The call pickup feature eliminates the need for the individual to answer a call in his or her own office. It also eliminates the need to have several lines on each telephone.

Individual Call Transfer **Individual call transfer** enables a user to transfer a call to another phone without an operator's help. This saves time for users and operators.

Conference Calling A **conference calling** service permits three or more persons to communicate on a single call. Some telephone systems enable you to make conference calls without operator assistance.

Caller ID **Caller ID** displays the number of an incoming call on a special panel or device. This panel or device is available through the telephone provider.

Call Trace **Call trace** determines the source of, or traces, the most recent incoming call. This service is helpful for tracing obscene or harassing phone calls.

Call Blocking **Call blocking** eliminates the display of your number on any Caller ID display device or panel.

TELEPHONE SECURITY AND SAFETY

In addition to becoming familiar with your telephone and its features, learn to use it safely. Practice these suggestions for the secure and safe use of your telephone.

1. **Keep any telephone away from water.** Water on or inside a phone—whether cord, cordless, or cellular—can cause an electrical shock. Avoid using a telephone near bathtubs, showers, swimming pools, Jacuzzis, and hot tubs. (See Figure 3-4.)

Figure 3-4 Avoid using phones near any water source because of the risk of electrical shock.

Figure 3-5 Avoid using phones during any type of catastrophe or weather that can directly affect telephone lines.

2. **Do not use any telephone during any type of catastrophe or weather that can directly affect telephone lines.** It is dangerous to use a telephone—whether cord, cordless, or cellular—during thundershowers, electrical storms, or natural disasters that affect phone lines. (See Figure 3-5.)

3. **If you receive a telephone call of a negative, obscene, or harassing nature, hang up.** Do not respond or raise your voice to telephone intruders. If such calls persist, report them promptly to your telephone provider. Report calls of a threatening nature immediately to the police and the telephone provider.

4. **Use caution when giving information over the telephone.** Many products and services are marketed over the telephone. Sometimes we receive these telemarketing calls at a most inconvenient time. Many of them are legitimate, but numerous others are scams or schemes to obtain information from you, such as a credit card number, address, type of household valuables, and names and number of family members.

   Do not allow a call of this type to go on needlessly and unwanted by you. Interrupt the caller and say you are not interested in the service or product. In addition, if you are hesitant to give credit card or other information over the telephone, request that the caller send you a brochure that explains the product or service. Remember, you are in charge of the call.

5. **Before allowing telephone repair technicians to enter your home, ask for and verify identification.** This helps to ensure your safety and demonstrates your awareness of security.

Figure 3-6 Verify the information on a telephone repairperson's ID tag. If necessary, call the stated telephone provider to confirm that person's employment.

TIME AND CHARGES

Time often costs money, especially on the telephone. Telephone charges can include the cost of the phone itself, features, services, and time used. These costs vary by company and situation.

Local calls may be billed per call, based on the length of the call. Local calls also may be billed at a flat monthly fee. Many providers bill one month in advance for local service.

Long-distance calls are billed separately from local calls. Rates for long-distance calls are based on several factors. These include the call's destination, day of the week, time of day, length of the conversation, and any operator services requested. Direct-dial long-distance calls cost less than operator-assisted calls. Operator-assisted calls made during the normal business day usually are the most costly.

Several companies offer long-distance services. Their rates are competitive and vary considerably. Before you select a long-distance company, consider the services you need and the cost of them.

ECONOMIZING LONG-DISTANCE CALLS

You can economize the cost of long-distance calls by doing the following:

- **Schedule lengthy long-distance calls in advance.** You will be more likely to reach the person you are calling. In addition, you might be able to call when rates are lower. Remember that rates are most expensive during normal business hours.

- **Schedule conference calls in advance.** All parties can be prepared when you plan ahead.

- **Use your telephone directory before calling directory assistance.** Avoid directory assistance charges by locating phone numbers yourself.

- **Get credit on your bill for service-related errors and problems.** Ask the operator for credit on calls that have poor connections (interference), calls that go through to wrong numbers, and loss of service.

Summary

1. Think about your telephone skills when you make a telephone call. An awareness of your skills will help you improve them.

2. Proper attitude is crucial to making a successful and positive telephone call.

3. Before you make a call, be mentally ready to initiate it and know the purpose of it.

4. Continue to plan the call as it progresses.

5. Have the necessary materials, such as account numbers, catalogs, and points to discuss, at your fingertips before you make the call.

6. Before you make a call, consider your own readiness and the time of day. Refer to the time zone map in your telephone directory to verify the time difference between your location and the recipient's.

7. If you cannot find a telephone number in a local, personal, or other telephone directory, call directory assistance for help.

8. A local telephone directory is sometimes called the *White Pages*. This directory provides an alphabetic listing of names and telephone numbers and other telephone reference information.

9. Use the *Yellow Pages* when you need to locate a product or service. If you cannot locate information on a particular topic in the *Yellow Pages*, search under related headings or subjects.

10. The first step in locating the telephone number of a business or residence is to know its name and its correct spelling.

11. A personal directory is your own record of frequently called numbers.

12. Most telephone directories include a list of the country codes and city codes for major foreign cities. These directories also explain how to make an international call. In addition to the codes, some directories list the time difference from a specific time zone to other countries.

13. Keep in mind that an extra charge is usually incurred whenever an operator is involved in your call.

14. Conference calls permit three or more parties to communicate on a single call, which saves time and costs.

15. Many telephone services are available and vary by geographic location.

16. Telephone charges can include the cost of the phone itself, features, services, and time used. These costs vary by company and situation.

Reinforcement Application 4

Using Your Telephone Directory

Directions: Use your local telephone directory to find the answers to the questions below. Write your answers in the spaces provided.

1. Which geographic region and area code(s) are covered by your local directory?

   _____

   _____

   _____

2. If you have a question concerning your telephone bill, what number should you call?

   _____

3. How would you call directory assistance for the state of West Virginia?

   _____

4. How would you call directory assistance for your local area?

   _____

5. If it is 4 p.m. in New York, what time is it in Arizona?

   _____

6. What is the area code for each city listed below?

   a. Freeport, Maine   _____

   b. Cincinnati, Ohio   _____

   c. Las Vegas, Nevada   _____

   d. San Juan, Puerto Rico   _____

7. What is the name of the time zone in which the state of Missouri is located?

   _____

8. What is the country code for each country listed below?

    a. Spain   _____

    b. New Zealand   _____

    c. Denmark   _____

    d. Mexico   _____

9. What is the city code for each city listed below?

    a. Barcelona, Spain   _____

    b. Wellington, New Zealand   _____

    c. Copenhagen, Denmark   _____

    d. Mexico City, Mexico   _____

10. List three community service groups that are listed in your telephone directory.

    _____

    _____

    _____

Reinforcement Application 5

Paying Less for More

Directions: Based on the information you have studied in Chapter 3, suggest ways to save money on each of the following calls.

1. Bob Kautz calls directory assistance at least 12 times a month for numbers that are listed in the telephone directory.

    _____

    _____

    _____

2. Ty Mongoluksana arranged a conference call at the last minute. Two of the five parties were unavailable, and the call had to be postponed.

    _____

    _____

    _____

3. Jameel Lord always rushes when he makes a call. Consequently, he frequently reaches an incorrect number and has to call again.

_____

_____

_____

_____

4. Sylvia Pease has known for nearly a week that she would have to speak with a supplier for at least an hour. The supplier is located a thousand miles away, and she makes a person-to-person call to make sure she reaches him.

_____

_____

_____

_____

5. Leo Aalborg frequently calls his mother long-distance during his lunch hour to chat. He charges the calls to his home telephone number.

_____

_____

_____

_____

Case Study 3

The Confused Caller

Directions: Analyze the situation described below. Then answer the questions that follow.

It's a late Monday afternoon, and you are waiting in the reception area of your dentist's office for your appointment. The dentist, Dr. Hatch, is running nearly 30 minutes behind on his appointments.

As you wait, you observe the receptionist, Valerie. Her desk is a mess, piled high with folders, copies of bills, checks, pens, envelopes, and Dr. Hatch's appointment book. Valerie's computer is positioned too high for her to sit comfortably at it. Each time the telephone rings—and it usually rings four times before Valerie answers it—she has to rummage around her desktop to find message forms and a pen that works. Often she needs Dr. Hatch's appointment book and cannot find it; when she does locate it, she has to go through several pages to locate the current month. In addition, as patients are arriving and leaving, it takes Valerie additional time to deal with them because of her disorganization.

Finally, Dr. Hatch appears and says, "Valerie, please call my appointments from 2 p.m. on and reschedule them. I will take care of the patients who are here, but I'm not feeling well. I just can't stay until 5 o'clock."

Valerie replies, "Yes, Dr. Hatch. I may not be able to reach all of them at this late hour, but I'll try."

Valerie begins to call the six patients who are scheduled from 2 p.m. on. For the next half hour, she is on the phone, trying to notify patients and reschedule their appointments. You notice that she has to locate the phone numbers within the patients' folders. Several of the folders are located in the mess on her desk. As she continues, she has difficulty reaching several patients because several of the home numbers do not have answering machines and she does not have their work numbers handy. In her growing anxiety, Valerie mistakenly calls two patients who do not have appointments that day. At the end of the half hour, she has reached only three of the six patients.

As Valerie pauses between calls, you ask her how much longer she thinks you will have to wait. You are already late getting back to work. Valerie offers to call your office and tell them you are delayed. Near the end of Valerie's conversation with your office, Dr. Hatch comes into the waiting room to ask why the next patient has not been sent in. In her confusion, Valerie hangs up her phone before ending the call. You leave, deciding to call at a later time to reschedule.

1. Why is the arrangement of Valerie's desk interfering with her ability to process calls?

   _____

   _____

   _____

   _____

   _____

   _____

2. What suggestions could you offer Valerie for improving the way she keeps track of telephone numbers?

   _____

   _____

   _____

   _____

   _____

   _____

3. What additional information about patients should Valerie record in order to be sure she can reach them during the working hours?

_____

_____

_____

_____

_____

4. How does Valerie's preoccupation with making the calls to patients affect her other job responsibilities?

_____

_____

_____

_____

_____

5. How do you think Valerie should have handled your problem concerning the lateness of your appointment?

_____

_____

_____

_____

_____

6. What should Valerie do to avoid reaching wrong numbers?

_____

_____

_____

_____

_____

7. What is your overall response to this case study?

_____

_____

_____

_____

_____

Managing Special Telephone Calls

OBJECTIVES

Chapter 4 will help you:

1. Develop your skill in managing special telephone calls: information request, appointment scheduling, complaint, collection, and telemarketing.

2. Reinforce and strengthen your questioning skills as you manage special telephone calls.

3. Understand that, whether you initiate or receive special telephone calls, having facts and accurate information handy reduces the need for repeat calls and promotes goodwill.

The telephone is often used for special kinds of telephone calls including information requests, appointment scheduling, complaint, collection, and telemarketing. You may not encounter all of these types of calls. However, if you learn to manage these calls in a timely and professional manner, you will increase your telephone productivity and effectiveness.

THE INFORMATION REQUEST CALL

The *information request* call involves giving and receiving information. In fact, one of the most common reasons to use the telephone is to request information because the telephone is a convenient and instantaneous medium.

OBTAINING INFORMATION

Before you make a call to obtain information, consider these questions:

- **WHOM** are you calling?

- **WHY** do you need the information?

- **WHAT** information do you need?

- **WHEN** do you need the information?

- **HOW** will the information be used?

Once this planning is completed, consider the important factors of making any telephone call: timing of the call, locating the correct telephone number, and making the most efficient type of call.

When obtaining information, be accurate and specific in what you request. Putting yourself in the place of the recipient will help you recognize that being professional and courteous throughout the call is important.

Putting yourself in the place of the recipient will help you recognize that being professional and courteous is important.

PLACING THE INFORMATION REQUEST CALL

When you place the information request call:

1. **Be prepared to identify yourself and your business, if appropriate.** Identify yourself appropriately before beginning the conversation.

   "Mr. Mealer, this is Anna Masonelle of Gruber Enterprises."

2. **Establish whether the timing of your call is convenient for the recipient.** Since you are requesting information, establish the convenience of the call. If the recipient feels a need to rush through your conversation because of another commitment, you may not have his or her undivided attention.

   "I would like additional information on the bid you submitted to us. Is this a convenient time to discuss it?"

3. **Give the recipient time to respond, and answer questions as completely as possible.** Allow the recipient to explain the answers to your questions. Likewise, answer questions of the recipient as completely as possible.

4. **Confirm the information you have received during the call, making sure that you understand what action, if any, needs to be taken.**

   "You'll deliver the revised bid to me next Wednesday."

5. **End the call courteously.** Thank the recipient for the information you received.

   "I'll look forward to discussing the bid with you late next week, Mr. Mealer. Thank you. Good-bye."

ACTIVITY 20: Obtaining Information Over the Telephone

The purpose of this activity is to help you determine what questions should be asked in order to obtain information via the telephone. It will also help you understand that planning the questions before the call is an excellent idea and a time-saver. Read each scenario below, then write an appropriate response.

1. Holly has decided that during her vacation she would like to visit her Aunt Justine, who lives in Fort Lauderdale, Florida. Holly, who lives in Omaha, Nebraska, wants to travel anytime between

February 14 and April 15. She would like information from Central Airlines concerning schedules and prices. What information should Holly request when she calls Central Airlines?

_____

_____

_____

_____

_____

_____

_____

_____

2. Kevin wants to purchase a new computer and printer. He plans to shop local stores and call out-of-state equipment centers that have a toll-free telephone number. What information should Kevin request regarding complete computer packages when he calls the equipment centers?

_____

_____

_____

_____

_____

_____

_____

_____

3. Nicky has chosen three scholarships for which she wants to apply. She has located their telephone numbers and wants to call for information. What questions should Nicky ask when she calls each site?

_____

_____

_____

_____

_____

_____

_____

_____

The purpose of this activity is to help you organize your thoughts before you speak in order to be clear. Read the statements below—some would be used to obtain information and others to provide it. Then, rewrite each statement in order to express clearly the needs of the speaker.

1. I really think I want some information about the conference, but I am not sure where to start—with the dates, the time, the location, the cost, or what.

   _____

   _____

   _____

   _____

2. Well . . . . I mean . . . . Oh gosh, I'm not sure of that date. I guess it is on Sunday at three, or maybe it is Tuesday at one. What should I do?

   _____

   _____

   _____

   _____

3. Someone told us North Main Street. I think that's the street we are looking for, or maybe it's South Main Street. Maybe the street is spelled M-a-i-n-e or it could be M-a-i-n-n-e or M-a-i-n. I just don't know.

   _____

   _____

   _____

   _____

4. There was a young man here to see you at about 2 this afternoon. He had on a navy blue suit, I think. He said he was looking for a check you had for him. I can't remember his name, but he had a business card he gave me. I think he was the one who gave me that business card. Where is it?

   _____

   _____

   _____

   _____

5. Our Internet class will not be meeting next week, Jean. I think she said we would meet at four the following week in Room 210. Or was it at three in Room 110? I thought I wrote it down on a slip of paper. I guess it actually was at four in Room 110. Yes, I think that's when it was.

_____

_____

_____

_____

PROVIDING INFORMATION

You will receive many information requests as you use and answer the telephone. In your job, you may be providing the same information repeatedly to callers; for example, you may work as an airline reservations agent or a customer service representative. (Customer service will be covered in Chapter 5.) If you know the information being requested, you will be better able to quickly and efficiently process these calls. Be prepared to respond to information requests in a positive, supportive, and respectful way.

RESPONDING TO THE INFORMATION REQUEST CALL

Follow these guidelines when giving information to callers.

1. **Respond promptly.** Some information can be given immediately; some information may require more time and research. Whatever the case, respond as quickly as possible. If you need time to find the information, tell the caller you will call back when the information is available.

   "I will need to check on the status of your payment and get back to you tomorrow."

2. **Be helpful.** Whenever you answer the telephone for your company, you represent yourself and the company. Your company relies on you to provide assistance to customers and the public. Your assistance helps to generate goodwill and possible new business.

   "I would be happy to check on the status of your order, Mr. Carlisle."

(continued on next page)

3. **Be accurate.** Listen carefully to the caller's request for information and respond with accurate information. If you need to verify the information, follow up with the caller.

   "The service department has thoroughly checked your computer. They found that the problem was one of the print drivers."

4. **Be complete.** Ask relevant questions so that you can give complete information when you respond to the caller.

   "I have checked the latest catalogs for the telephone equipment you specified. I am pleased to report that we can offer you several packages at very competitive prices."

5. **Plan what you will do when you are not sure what to do.** If you are not sure of what to do or say when someone is requesting information, put the caller on hold and ask your supervisor for help. If help is not available, tell the caller you will return the call to give an answer as soon as possible. Alternatively, you might want to transfer the caller to a person who can provide the requested information.

   "Unfortunately, I will not be able to give you an answer today, but I will get back to you within two days after I have done more research."

6. **Say "no" in a positive manner.** When you are not able to provide what the caller wants, be firm but courteous and professional.

   "It looks as if I will not be able to help you at this time but may be able to as soon as the new catalog arrives."

7. **End the call courteously.** Express appreciation for the call, whether or not you fulfilled the information request.

   "Thank you for calling, Ms. Weinsteger. I hope we can be of service to you again in the near future."
   "Thank you for calling, Mr. Henshaw. Perhaps we will be better able to help you next month, when our updated catalog arrives."

THE APPOINTMENT SCHEDULING CALL

Calls for *appointment scheduling* require you to be specific in obtaining and recording complete information. In an appointment scheduling call, you make or schedule an appointment. When you schedule appointments for yourself or for another person or company, you may wish to use a few simple strategies to save you time and money.

When scheduling appointments, have a calendar nearby to assist you in verifying dates and times. Printed or electronic appointment calendars are available in a variety of formats. If you are scheduling appointments for another person, have that person's calendar handy. (See Figure 4-2.) Once you have scheduled appointments for yourself or another person, write a reminder of the appointments. This reminder should be complete and can include the following:

Never rely upon your memory—or force others to rely upon it—for details. Write appointment details on paper, or enter them in an electronic calendar.

- Name of the patient, client, or customer

- Exact address and telephone number of the patient, client, or customer

- Day, date, place, and time of appointment

- Purpose of and/or other details of the appointment

- Name of the person who made the appointment (if other than yourself)

- Identification of the caller including file number, account number, or case number (if appropriate, as in a doctor's, accountant's, or attorney's office)

Likewise, the caller needs to know the following information about the appointment:

- Name of person to be seen

- Exact date and time of appointment

- Location of appointment, with detailed directions

- Special instructions

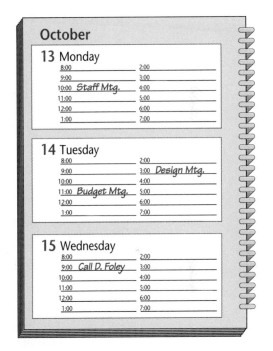

Figure 4-2

Some offices that schedule appointments regularly call the patient, client, or customer one day before the appointment to confirm it. A missed appointment may result in a fee to the patient, client, or customer.

The purpose of this activity is to learn that scheduling appointments involves obtaining and recording complete information. Margaret wrote the following notes when scheduling appointments for her two managers, Sahana and Clay. Analyze the information given for each appointment to determine if it is complete. If the information is complete, write OK in the space provided; if it is not, indicate what is missing.

1. For Sahana,

   Marcia McNeil will see you concerning the service contract for equipment. Her number is 555-9080. The appointment is scheduled for Wednesday, March 14, at 11 a.m. in your office.

   _____

   _____

   _____

2. For Clay,

   Bernice Kinney and Brooke Terrone will see you on March 13 at 9 a.m. I have scheduled Conference Room B for the meeting.

   _____

   _____

   _____

3. For Clay,

   Peter Reardon will be in on Thursday, March 15, to see you.

   _____

   _____

   _____

4. For Sahana,

   Dewaine Craig and Nundi Romano are coming in for a one-hour appointment at 10 a.m. in your office. They want to discuss some marketing tips with you.

   _____

   _____

5. For Clay,

   Brenda Buzzell will be coming to meet with you at 2 p.m. on Monday, March 12. She wants to talk to you about planning a retirement party for a colleague. Her number is 201-555-8796.

   _____

   _____

ASSESSMENT 3: Your Readiness To Schedule Appointments

Are you appropriately prepared to schedule appointments? Complete the checklist below, trying to be as objective as you can. After you analyze your findings, determine three areas on which you need to improve when scheduling appointments.

	Always	Usually	Need Improvement
1. Do I have the appropriate appointment book(s) handy when I schedule appointments?	_____	_____	_____
2. Am I prepared to listen attentively to the caller for all details concerning scheduling the appointment?	_____	_____	_____
3. Do I have forms available to record messages and other details related to scheduling appointments?	_____	_____	_____
4. Do I offer alternatives for scheduling, if necessary?	_____	_____	_____
5. Do I verify the details of the scheduled appointment by repeating to the caller the day, date, and time of the appointment as well as the caller's telephone number?	_____	_____	_____
6. Do I clarify any points of confusion in connection with the call?	_____	_____	_____
7. Do I call and confirm the appointment the day before it is to be held?	_____	_____	_____
8. Do I know the time when I confirm a scheduled appointment?	_____	_____	_____

THE COMPLAINT CALL

A *complaint* call can present many challenges because it involves some type of problem or mistake. In doing business, people make mistakes, suffer the consequences of mistakes, or simply think and feel that they have been wronged. Whether you are making a call to complain or responding to someone's complaint over the telephone, you must deal with facts and sometimes powerful feelings or emotions.

MAKING COMPLAINTS

The word *complain* denotes a negative undertone and causes most people to react with negative feelings, such as frustration, annoyance, or anger. Control your negative feelings before making the call. Concentrate on the facts of the situation and make sure that the mistake you think was made actually did occur.

For example, suppose you placed a special order for software that would allow you to complete a project. When you unpacked the order, you found that you received the wrong version of the software. Before you become angry, check your record of the order and the packing slip. If you did receive the wrong version of the software, you are correct to call and complain about the situation.

Once you have the facts correct, are calm, and have all the information handy, make the complaint call. Remember, your goal is to resolve the problem. You need to be firm, yet tactful, courteous, and professional.

Figure 4-3 Control your negative feelings when making a complaint call.

MAKING A COMPLAINT CALL

Remember these suggestions for expressing your needs when you have to make a complaint call.

1. **Be courteous.** Do not demand to speak to the manager, accuse inappropriately, or imply that the listener cannot help you. Instead, describe the problem briefly and ask who can help you resolve it. Politeness will more likely result in an acceptable solution.

   "This is Whitney Tulles. I would like to speak to someone about a shipment I received today."

2. **Describe the error impersonally.** Use of the word you assigns blame for the error. Avoid using you by wording your remarks in the passive, not active, voice. Your goal is to keep the other person feeling positive and willing to help you.

   Don't say: "You didn't send me the correct version of software!"
   Do say: "It looks as if the wrong version of software was sent."

3. **Suggest a solution that would be satisfactory to you.** Have a possible solution in mind. If your suggestion is reasonable, the other party may be more willing to consider it.

   "Could you please send me the correct version of the software by overnight mail without extra charge. I need it tomorrow."

4. **End the call courteously.** If you have been positive throughout the call, end the call courteously, making sure you thank the recipient.

   "Thank you for your help. I'll look forward to receiving the correct software tomorrow morning."

The purpose of this activity is to manage information request and complaint calls with professionalism and courtesy. The statements below are responses that a recipient gave to callers. Read each response. If the response was professional and courteous, write OK in the space provided. If it was not professional and courteous, rewrite the statement.

1. Well, Mr. Chin, that is the way that meeting agenda has to be!

   _____

   _____

   _____

2. Thank you for calling, Miss Bordeaux. I will be in touch with you soon.

   _____

   _____

   _____

3. The advertising campaign will not be changed. That involves too much work to rearrange everything at this late time in the marketing season.

   _____

   _____

   _____

4. I am sorry that we had you scheduled on the wrong flight. I can arrange for you to be picked up at the airport by one of our representatives. Would that help you?

   _____

   _____

   _____

5. We can provide that information. However, I must warn you that it will cost you quite a bit of money, because you know our time is valuable and it will take a lot of time to research our database.

   _____

   _____

   _____

6. I will be glad to send that book right out to you if you will provide me with the necessary information.

_____

_____

_____

7. The meeting will not be taking place. You can call to find out when it will be rescheduled; we can't afford to call you.

_____

_____

_____

8. The items you are requesting were delivered to our warehouse last Thursday, but we haven't had time to inventory them yet. What do you expect of us?

_____

_____

_____

9. I expect to have that answer within the hour. I will be glad to call and leave a message on your voice mail, if you wish.

_____

_____

_____

10. I don't understand why you are upset. Why couldn't you call us? We have had so many applications to process that we certainly can't call everyone!

_____

_____

_____

RESPONDING TO COMPLAINTS

Unfortunately, many people voice complaints in negative ways over the telephone. Such experiences can cause you to lose control and react angrily to the caller. Applying the following important points will help you manage these complaint calls:

MANAGING COMPLAINT CALLS

1. **Answer the telephone promptly and identify yourself properly.** Answer the phone in a pleasant, helpful manner. Identify yourself appropriately and offer to assist the caller.

   "Superintendent's office; this is Nikki. How may I help you?"

2. **Ask open-ended questions.** Be respectful of the caller's feelings, but try to maintain control of the conversation. Redirect the caller's attention from feelings to the facts of the situation. Ask open-ended questions to help you determine the nature of the problem.

   "What is the nature of the defect?"

3. **Confirm your understanding of the problem.** An emotional caller can confuse the facts, making it difficult for you to understand the situation. If necessary, politely ask the caller to repeat the problem. Once you think you understand the facts, confirm them with the caller to make sure that you both understand the problem.

   "Okay, Mrs. Lyons, let me be sure I understand the problem. You ordered one headboard in antique blue, and you received one headboard in antique brown. Is that correct?"

4. **Be helpful and offer solutions.** If it is clear that you or your company is in error, apologize for the error and the inconvenience it caused. If you can, offer a solution to the caller's problem or agree to a solution that is reasonable.

5. **End the call courteously and positively.** Leave the caller feeling positive about you, your company, and the results of the call.

THE COLLECTION CALL

In a *collection call*, the caller's goal is to collect money for an account balance by getting a commitment from the recipient to pay. Collection agencies train employees how to make collection calls. Even without the training, though, you may need to place collection calls. If you are placed in such a position, keep these important points in mind.

Collecting money for overdue payments can disturb the recipient. Treat the recipient respectfully—without insulting— and courteously.

MAKING COLLECTION CALLS

Use these guidelines when making collection calls.

1. **Identify yourself properly and establish the convenience of the call.** Be positive, especially when collecting money over the telephone. The call will not be pleasant to the recipient, so be sure that the recipient has time to speak with you. Be aware that some recipients may know what the call is about and put off talking to you.

   "Hello, Mr. Chin. This is Anna from AutoMart. Is this a good time to speak with you?"

2. **State your purpose clearly and directly.** Be direct to maintain control of the conversation.

   "I am calling about your account balance with us."

   "I am calling about your past-due account balance."

3. **Listen to the recipient's response.** Allow the recipient to explain the delay involving the account payment. Take precise notes.

4. **Request prompt action on the part of the recipient.** Get a commitment regarding payment from the recipient. Whenever possible, request payment in terms of the needs, interests, and pride of the recipient.

   "Can you make a partial payment now and send the remaining balance within thirty days?"

   "You've always paid on time in the past. How soon do you expect to be able to clear your present balance?"

5. **End the call courteously, repeating the action to be taken by the recipient.** Thank the recipient and repeat the payment arrangement for clarification.

   "Thank you, Mr. Chin. We'll look forward to receiving your check for $500 before July 1. Good-bye."

6. **Record your conversation so that you can follow up after a reasonable amount of time has elapsed.** Document conversations to provide proof of discussions and outline possible future actions.

THE TELEMARKETING CALL

Telemarketing is the process of using the telephone to market or sell a product or service. It is an efficient and cost-effective means to market and sell a wide variety of products and services.

Some of the more common uses of telemarketing include the following:

- Targeting sales leads
- Reaching customers worldwide
- Using time in the selling process more effectively
- Obtaining instant feedback on products or services

THE TELEMARKETER

Telemarketers usually are very knowledgeable about the product or service being marketed. They must have excellent oral communication skills, quick decision-making abilities, and strong listening skills.

Telemarketers must reflect a positive attitude, have a pleasant voice, and be persistent but not overly aggressive. Good telemarketers with the proper attitude can yield great profits for businesses.

Telemarketers often work for companies that provide telemarketing services for clients. Some may work in the marketing department of the company that sells the product or service.

THE TELEMARKETING SETTING

These factors help to promote a safe and positive setting for selling over the telephone:

- **A room that is adequately temperature-controlled.** Trying to sell over the telephone in a room that is too hot or too cold adversely affects a positive attitude.

- **An ergonomic environment.** Furniture, including a chair and table or desk, should be comfortable. Equipment, such as a computer screen, keyboard, and telephone, should be appropriately positioned. Lighting should be adequate.

- **Up-to-date telephone system.** The telephone system should be current with modern technology and features. Employees should be thoroughly trained to use the equipment efficiently.

- **Support.** The telemarketer must be supported by a supervisor who can handle unusual problems that might arise.

MAKING A TELEMARKETING CALL

Follow these guidelines when making a telemarketing call.

1. **Be sure you reach the right person.** As the telemarketer, you may reach a receptionist who screens calls. Your goal is to be forwarded to the potential customer or client. Be self-confident and courteous.

Receptionist: "Good afternoon, Dearborn Office Center. May I help you?"

Telemarketer: "Yes, hopefully you can. This is Myra Burbank calling from Park Associates in San Francisco. May I speak with Dean Perry?"

Receptionist: "I'm sorry. Mr. Perry is not available at the moment. Could someone else help you?"

Telemarketer: "Perhaps. I'm following up on a previous call to Mr. Perry about his interest in several new office chairs."

Receptionist: "Perhaps Ms. Chan could help you; she handles equipment purchases. Would you like to speak with her?"

Telemarketer: "That would be fine. Thank you."

The telemarketer was polite at all times, even when she was told Mr. Perry was unavailable. She succeeded in being forwarded to someone who might have the authority to make purchases.

2. **Generate interest.** At the beginning of the call, tell the prospect the reason for your call. Indicate possible benefits for listening to your message. You may mention a mutual acquaintance who provided the prospect's name. Ask a few questions to determine if the prospect is interested.

Telemarketer: "Ms. Hunter, this is Tim Spisak. Your name was given to me by Constance Long. She thought you might be interested in hearing more about a new type of desktop publishing software we are selling. She mentioned that you have your own home-based consulting business where you use desktop publishing. Is that true?"

Ms. Hunter: "Yes, I do have my own business here in my home, and I do quite a bit of desktop publishing."

Telemarketer:	"Well, if you could spare about five minutes, I'd like to explain how this new desktop publishing software can help you."
Ms. Hunter:	"Fine, as long as it's only five minutes. I have a meeting to go to in ten minutes."

If Ms. Hunter had indicated she was not interested, the telemarketer could have asked two or three more questions to generate interest. If there still was no interest, the call would be ended. Since Ms. Hunter indicated that she was interested, the telemarketer presented the product.

3. **Make the sales presentation.** Once the prospect is interested, and he or she has given the time to talk with you, describe the product or service. Tell the prospect about one or two major benefits he or she would enjoy about your product or service.

4. **Overcome objections.** As a telemarketer, you can expect potential customers to raise objections to the sales presentation. You may plan your responses ahead of time, usually using a prepared script. If you cannot overcome the prospect's objections, or if for each objection you overcome, the prospect thinks of another, thank the prospect for speaking with you and end the call.

5. **Secure the sale.** If you overcome the objections raised by the potential customer, ask for the order immediately. One way to do this is to ask a forced-choice question.

   "Would you prefer to order the oak or cherry desk?"

6. **Confirm the order.** If the customer agreed to purchase your product or service, verify the name, address, payment information, and the details of the order. Read this information back to the customer.

7. **End the call courteously.** End the call courteously, thanking the customer and saying good-bye.

Summary

1. One of the most common reasons to use the telephone is to make an information request because the telephone is a convenient and instantaneous medium.

2. When obtaining information, be accurate and specific in what you request.

3. Quickly determine what information is being requested so you can quickly and efficiently process an information request call.

4. When scheduling appointments, have a calendar nearby to assist you in verifying dates and times.

5. A complaint call can present many challenges because it involves some type of problem or mistake.

6. Control your negative feelings before making a complaint call.

7. Be positive, especially when collecting money over the telephone.

8. Telemarketing is the most popular way to market and sell a wide variety of products and services today because it is efficient and cost-effective.

9. Telemarketers must have excellent oral communication skills, quick decision-making abilities, and strong listening skills. They must reflect a positive attitude, have a pleasant voice, and be persistent but not overly aggressive.

Reinforcement Application 6

Practicing Positive Responses

Directions: Read each of the following responses from a telephone conversation. Determine if each is positive and courteous. If it is, place a check mark in the Yes column. If it is not, place a check mark in the No column, then rewrite the response to make it positive.

	Yes	No
1. "I sent you my bill over five weeks ago, and you still haven't sent me a check yet."	_____	_____

_____

_____

_____

2. "It would be extremely helpful if you would provide me with that information." _____ _____

_____

_____

_____

3. "McDonald & Martin, Sarah here. Hold on." _____ _____

_____

_____

_____

4. "You must have asked for the hooded sweatshirt. It says so right here on my copy of the order." _____ _____

_____

_____

_____

5. "I don't have time to check that right now." _____ _____

_____

_____

_____

6. "Thank you for calling, Mrs. Rankin. We appreciate your bringing that problem to our attention." _____ _____

_____

_____

_____

7. "The Telecommunications Department must have made another mistake. Hold on, I'll transfer you." _____ _____

_____

_____

_____

8. "I don't know what you are talking about." _____ _____

_____

_____

_____

9. "That's not my job." _____ _____

_____

_____

_____

10. "I'm not interested in having it fixed! I want a new one." _____ _____

_____

_____

_____

Case Study 4

The Inexperienced Telemarketer

Directions: Analyze the situation described below and then answer the questions that follow. Try to provide answers that reflect your understanding of the concepts you learned in Chapter 4.

Ryan Keelman has been hired to telemarket advertising space in a new weekly community newspaper. Ryan's previous telemarketing experience was with a large marketing firm. That experience covered all aspects of the marketing process, including prospects, scripts, product information, and procedures.

The newspaper hopes that with Ryan's experience, he should be able to start selling right away. Ryan feels a great deal of pressure, so he picks up the local *Yellow Pages* and immediately starts making calls. The first day presents many challenges. First, he selects businesses to call that rarely advertise in the local paper. Second, when he does reach someone who might be interested, he doesn't have enough information to answer questions. Third, he can't think of reasons why the prospect should advertise with the paper he represents rather than the established competitor. As a result, he makes only one minor sale that day.

The next day Ryan arrives at work and realizes he has to plan before making any calls.

1. Why is Ryan having difficulty reaching appropriate prospects when he makes calls randomly?

_____

_____

_____

_____

2. How could a telemarketing script help Ryan manage his tele-marketing calls?

_____

_____

_____

_____

3. What information should be contained in a telemarketing script to help Ryan during his calls?

_____

_____

_____

_____

Customer Service on the Telephone

OBJECTIVES

Chapter 5 will help you:

1. Use the telephone effectively to provide and receive customer service.

2. Focus on the importance your voice plays in providing quality customer service.

3. Strengthen your listening skills while delivering quality customer service.

4. Use appropriate questioning techniques when delivering quality customer service.

5. Appreciate the role technology plays in delivering quality customer service over the telephone.

Serving customers is a primary focus for businesses. *Customer service* is the management and follow-up of customers' questions, concerns, and complaints regarding products and/or services. Because of the convenience of using the telephone, customer service often is managed over the telephone, instead of face-to-face. These calls are managed by the *customer service professional*, or customer service representative.

Positive customer service is important in establishing goodwill in any business. A business with a poor-quality customer service department may lose clients and business, sometimes permanently. Everyone with whom you come in contact is a potential customer. Provide service to them that will meet their needs positively and invite them to continue doing business with you. Customers often provide good ideas to help a business improve its customer service. Value and respect your customer's needs.

PROVIDING AND RECEIVING QUALITY CUSTOMER SERVICE

You must provide ongoing quality customer service in order to keep your customers. Usually only a small number of customers complain. However, that small number can do much damage to the reputation of your personal performance and your business.

Poor customer service occurs for many reasons, such as:

- Lack of interest in a customer's individual needs.
- Poor decision-making.
- Use of ineffective communication skills with customers.
- Little or poor training in customer service.

This chapter will provide guidelines to help you provide and receive quality customer service.

Maintaining Voice Quality

Use your voice to convey a positive message to the customer.

Your voice is very important in providing and receiving quality customer service. Your voice can convey messages by its pitch, tone, and speed. The way you speak over the telephone creates a picture of yourself. Think about how your telephone personality translates to a customer who is unhappy or to someone trying to locate information.

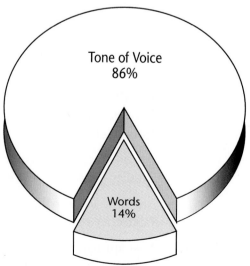

Figure 5-1 The tone of voice you use in a conversation has more effect than the actual words.

ASSESSMENT 4: Your Customer Service Voice on the Telephone

How professional is your voice when delivering expert customer service on the telephone? Place a check mark next to each statement below that applies to your voice.

_____ 1. My voice has a pleasant pitch that is not offensive.

_____ 2. I articulate dialects and accents clearly and accurately.

_____ 3. I tend to pause too much when I am speaking.

_____ 4. My rate of speech is normal.

_____ 5. I try to adjust the volume of my voice when necessary.

_____ 6. I always try to convey a smile in my voice.

_____ 7. The tone of my voice usually indicates that I am actively listening.

_____ 8. The tone of my voice is positive when I am speaking with customers over the telephone.

_____ 9. My voice often is either too loud or too soft, depending on my mood.

_____ 10. My voice is louder when I try to speak faster when dealing with customers over the telephone.

How did you rate? For any voice assessments that you felt were unprofessional or negative, begin working to improve them. Ask your instructor for suggestions.

You may provide customer service to someone with a dialect or an accent that differs from yours. The way you speak will determine whether you will communicate with your customer positively. Be aware of your telephone voice quality, and work to improve it if necessary.

MAINTAINING VOICE QUALITY

Keep the following points in mind to help you maintain your voice quality on the telephone:

- **Maintain a tone that is positive, clear, and enthusiastic.** This makes the customer interested.

- **Create comfortable conversation.** Customer service professionals, or representatives, often use scripts that help them to create a positive voice quality.

- **Use a vocabulary that is easy to understand.** This creates a relaxed, positive atmosphere. The way you emphasize certain words can contribute to delivering quality customer service, instead of poor customer service.

- **Keep a smile on your face.** In fact, check your smile in a mirror periodically to remind you how important it is!

ACTIVITY 24: Using the Right Words With Customers

The purpose of this activity is to help you understand how your voice can emphasize certain words, changing a customer's perception for the better or worse.

Read each sentence below—if possible, with a partner. Emphasize with your voice the words in bold print. (Notice that each sentence is identical, with different words being emphasized.) Write a comment about each sentence, giving your reaction to the words being emphasized and the different effects each phrase has in relation to practicing good customer service.

1. **How** may I help you?
2. How may I **help** you?

_____

_____

_____

3. **Unfortunately**, our supply of that item is totally exhausted.
4. Unfortunately, our supply of that item is **totally** exhausted.

_____

_____

_____

5. What is the **best** time to return your call?
6. What is the best time to **return** your call?

_____

_____

_____

7. **Thank you** for that information; I will get back to you shortly.
8. Thank you for that information; I will get **back** to you shortly.

_____

_____

_____

9. Let's **verify** that date—that's Monday, November 23.
10. Let's verify that date—that's **Monday, November 23**.

_____

_____

_____

Establishing Proper Identification

You may encounter special challenges when you try to reach a specific person. Study this example:

Professional: "Is this the home of Donna DuBouis?"

Recipient: "Yes, it is."

Professional: "May I please speak with her?"

Recipient: "I'm sorry, Donna is not here right now. Could you speak with someone else or could I take a message?"

Professional: "No, I will call again. Thank you."

In the preceding example, the caller wanted to contact a specific person but was unsuccessful in doing so. You may not always reach the correct person in each call. Be polite to the person who answers the phone to help ensure the success of future calls made to that business or residence.

In the following conversation, the representative does reach the customer.

Professional: "Good morning. May I speak to Molly Lyons?"

Recipient: "This is Molly Lyons."

Professional: "Molly, how are you? This is Michael from the Frame Factory. I am calling concerning your problem with a frame we made for you. Is this a good time to speak with you?"

The caller established proper identification with the recipient. The caller was polite, the recipient knew the purpose of the call, and the caller established the convenience of the call.

ACTIVITY 25: Answers To Customer Service Calls

The purpose of this activity is to learn to make and receive customer service calls correctly. Read each scenario below, analyzing each for correct procedure concerning answering and making calls. Then respond to the questions.

Scenario 1

The All Points South Travel Agency in Salt Lake City, Utah, has expanded to include a subdivision dealing with international travel. All agents have been assigned specific areas to cover. The phone rings, and Jon picks up the phone. The customer is interested in booking a trip to the New England area. Jon knows the customer and would like to help her, but he knows he has been assigned a new area. Jon tells the customer, "Mrs. Valentina, I no longer schedule trips within the United States. However, I will be happy to transfer your call to the correct department if you will please hold."

1. a. Is Jon practicing good telephone procedure?

   _____ Yes   _____ No

   b. Comments:

   _____

   _____

   _____

Scenario 2

Marilee is trying to contact the Director of Admissions at Andoverville College. The receptionist answers the telephone by saying, "Andoverville College, may I help you?"
Marilee states that she would like to speak to the Director of Admissions.
The receptionist asks, "Who is calling?" After Marilee states her name, the receptionist replies, "I am sorry, the director is not in today. Do you want to leave a message?"

2. a. Is the receptionist practicing good telephone customer service?

_____ Yes   _____ No

b. Comments:

_____

_____

_____

Scenario 3

Kirstiana is just finishing up her weekly report on customer service calls. Her telephone is ringing repeatedly. After about eight rings, she answers it, "Hello!"
It is a customer who is calling concerning a problem with a rental car.
Kirstiana is extremely frustrated and replies, "I'm sorry. I can't speak with you just now. Could you call back Monday?"

3. a. How would you rate Kirstiana's customer service over the telephone ?

_____ Acceptable   _____ Unacceptable

b. Comments:

_____

_____

_____

Answering Techniques

If you are answering the telephone, as opposed to making the call, keep the following points in mind.

1. **Answer the telephone on the first or second ring.** If the phone continues to ring, the caller will not appreciate your lateness and could feel neglected.

2. **Provide your name and any other appropriate identification.** The identification may include your department, division, or unit.

    "Customer Service; this is Ryan. How may I help you?"

    "Book Department. Mrs. Hodges speaking."

Smile when talking on the telephone. It makes your voice sound pleasant.

3. **Smile when you answer the telephone.** A smile relaxes your vocal chords. You might want to put a sign with the word "smile" on it near your telephone as a reminder.

Listening Actively

Active listening is important to communicating effectively with customers. Many of the listening concepts you learned in Chapter 1 also apply to customer service. Several other considerations are directly targeted at customer service calls. When you talk with customers, listen to their needs. Do not immediately launch into the conversation.

LISTENING ACTIVELY

Keep the following points in mind to listen actively when providing quality customer service.

Listen carefully to the concerns and needs of customers. Are they angry or are they simply clarifying a point?

Determine what your reaction will be to the situation. Remember, the customer is always right—whether or not that is true!

Indicate your willingness to listen to the needs of your customer. Use reinforcing words, such as "I see" or "I understand." This will let your customer know that you are concerned and are listening.

Record the major points of the discussion with customers. Documentation is important. It can help you assess the situation, repeat concerns, or determine what action will please the customer.

Remember, listening is a skill that must be practiced constantly. Eliminate poor listening habits so that you can serve your customer efficiently and effectively.

Asking Questions

Ask the right questions to carry out customer service effectively. Expert customer service centers around questions. The questions should help you provide service for your customers with a personal, helpful style.

Background questions help you to direct your caller to the correct department or person, or to obtain important information to serve the customer.

"I see, Mr. Martin. Will you please answer several questions so I can try to handle your problem immediately."

The open question, as described in Chapter 1, requires more of an answer than *yes* or *no*. Use the open question to help you explore the problem the customer is having, to identify major issues, and to determine possible solutions.

"Could you explain the situation to me, please?"

"What do you think should be your next course of action?"

The *verification question*, or confirmation question, verifies or confirms that information provided is correct or understood.

"How do you feel about trying that approach?"

"May I assume, then, that you are willing to go along with that for the moment?"

ACTIVITY 26: Listening to Your Customers' Needs

The purpose of this activity is to learn to listen to your customers' needs. Customers are not always direct in stating their needs. Sometimes you need to get more information from them before you can help them.

Read each statement below to understand what the customer needs. If you understood the customer's needs, place a check mark in the Yes column. If you did not understand the customer's needs, place a check mark in the No column. Then explain specifically your reason for not understanding.

	Yes	No
1. Your customer screamed at you over the telephone about how uneducated the staff must be in your company.	_____	_____

_____

_____

_____

2. Your customer was polite, friendly, and knew that she wanted the yellow drape to be replaced with a blue drape, No. 793GA, of the same size.

_____   _____

_____

_____

_____

3. When your customer indicated some negativism concerning your promotion, you replied in a pleasant manner, trying a positive approach.

_____   _____

_____

_____

_____

4. Your customer spoke to you in garbled tones, as if she had something in her mouth. You could hear a lot of background music and other noise.

_____   _____

_____

_____

_____

TECHNOLOGY AND CUSTOMER SERVICE

Voice Mail, Answering Machines, and Pagers

Answering devices, such as voice mail, answering machines, and pagers, are important in telephone technology today. Whether a person or an answering device is available to answer incoming calls depends on the size of the business and the number of customer service professionals available.

Answering devices can increase productivity and serve customers better if customer service representatives return calls to customers who have left messages.

Customer service professionals recognize that placing a message on voice mail or an answering machine can create a gap between them and their customers. Because of this gap, the possibility exists that the customer and the professional may never get in touch with each other. On the other hand, when customer service representatives leave messages on answering machines or voice mail, they show that they care and have taken the time to show personal interest in customers.

The use of voice mail raises concerns by those who work with customer service. Some businesses feel that the personal touch is lost when customers have to speak into voice mail. Others view it as a way to retain goodwill when people are unavailable to speak on the telephone.

Some customer service numbers connect the customer to a recording. This recording may offer a selection of several options that help serve the customer. These recordings usually offer a code that the customer can select to hear the message repeated. The recordings also may have an option (usually by pressing 0) that bypasses the message and allows the caller to speak to a person. Customers can become frustrated quickly when they reach a prerecorded message, have to make several selections, and perhaps never speak to an actual person.

Pagers, or *beepers*, are small, portable devices that beep or vibrate to notify you that someone has called your pager number. Pagers may be carried or worn, such as in a pocket or on a belt. Pagers can improve customer service because they instantly notify the user of a call. This is especially important when the user is unreachable by phone.

Some pagers record only the caller's number on the pager display. Others allow the caller to record a message. This message can be accessed by the user with a phone call to a special number.

Pagers usually work only within a certain geographic range. A caller may not be able to reach a pager unless it is within range. Mobile individuals should make alternate arrangements for receiving messages.

USING ANSWERING DEVICES

Remember the following points when using voice mail, answering machines, and pagers.

- **Establish a plan for paging.** You may be able to reach pager users by phone at certain times of the day. Therefore, know what circumstances require you to page the user; for example, emergency situations or when the individual is mobile.

- **Carry your pager with you at all times.** It will be difficult to communicate with you if your pager is left elsewhere.

- **Change your voice mail, answering machine, or pager message periodically to keep the information current.** Record professional messages. Likewise, use messages that are current and meet customers' needs.

"Hello, you have reached Nathan Woloszyn of Doe Communications. If you are calling from the western territory, please contact Angela Lytle at 609-555-7888; I no longer service that area. If you are calling from the southeastern territory, please leave your name, telephone number, and a brief message. I will be glad to return your call as soon as possible."

- **Write your message for incoming calls before recording it.** Write your message that will answer incoming calls. Review it for clarity before you record it.

  "Hello, you have reached Selena Dobrachav of A-1 Engineering. I am traveling out of the office on business May 11–14 and will be returning on May 15. Please leave your name, telephone number, and a brief message so that I may return your call. Thank you."

- **Speak clearly and intelligibly.** When you record or leave a message on any answering device, enunciate your words and form a clear message.

  "This is Sam Bright of Bright Enterprises. Please call me at 614-555-7824 on Tuesday, June 3, between 8 a.m. and 1 p.m. about the amendment to the Brigson contract."

ACTIVITY 27: Leaving Messages for Customers

The purpose of this activity is to help you learn whether it is appropriate to leave a message for a customer. Read each statement below and determine whether a message should be left for the customer if he or she is unavailable. If a message should be left, place a check mark in the Yes column. If a message should not be left, place a check mark in the No column. Explain your answers.

	Yes	No
1. You want to tell a potential customer about the services of your advertising company. You hope he might be interested.	_____	_____
2. You are returning a call to one of your customers who called you earlier today. She is having a problem with the new printer she purchased recently from your company.	_____	_____

_____

_____

3. You are finishing up a sales campaign. The person you are calling bought a lot of office supplies from you during another sales campaign. You feel strongly that he might be interested in doing so again. The sales campaign will end in three days.   _____ _____

_____

_____

_____

_____

4. You want one of your regular customers to call you today to finalize an order that needs to be processed by the end of the day.   _____ _____

_____

_____

_____

_____

5. You have previously called this potential customer and left a message, but no one ever returned your call. You know this customer is very interested in your products. You have information about a special offer that you feel this person could take advantage of.   _____ _____

_____

_____

_____

_____

The Internet

In today's world, the Internet, e-mail, and the World Wide Web are being used more and more to purchase many products and services. These technologies also are being used to report and respond to customer service needs. These topics will be covered in greater detail in Chapter 6.

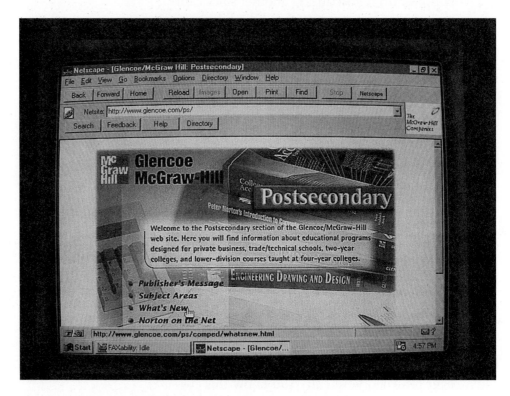

Figure 5-2 Some companies provide customer service options on Internet home pages.

UNDERSTANDING CUSTOMER NEEDS

All customers have basic needs that you must be prepared to meet as a customer service professional.

- They need to be treated pleasantly.

- They need to be treated professionally throughout the entire call.

- They need to be offered possible solutions to their problems or concerns.

Reading Your Customer's Mind

With customer service training and some experience, you will learn to "read" your customer's mind. You will find that most customers want to be treated fairly and professionally whatever the situation. Often you will be able to predict the outcome that the customer wants.

Customers do not like to fill out extensive surveys and write long answers. Similarly, they do not like to provide long answers or explanations over the telephone. In both situations, customers respond well to questions that are direct and require a simple answer.

Dealing with Objections

Ideally, all customer service calls would yield positive responses. Realistically, objections do occur, and sometimes the caller is not interested in responding positively to a customer service representative. When a customer raises an objection, you must handle the situation quickly and effectively. If you do not, you could lose a customer or a potential customer.

Listening is the key to managing objections. You must understand what you are hearing from your customer and know what you can say to help overcome the objection.

DEALING WITH CUSTOMER OBJECTIONS

Keep these points in mind as you deal with customer objections.

- **Control your emotions.** Perhaps there is a reason why the customer is demonstrating a particular emotion. Listen to the customer carefully, and keep your emotions under control.

- **Determine what is the major objection, and deal with that particular one.** Use good questioning techniques to help you manage the call and establish good customer service.

- **Reply to the customer in a positive tone, and respond only to the specific objection.** Do not waiver from the discussion.

- **Offer possible solutions.** Try to work out an acceptable solution for both you and your customer.

- **End the call professionally.** As always, be positive and express appreciation for the call.

CUSTOMER SERVICE TIPS

What are some things you can do to promote effective customer service? The following tips apply whether you are working with customer service outside your business or within your business.

1. **Follow up with all customers on a regular basis.** Follow-up may be by telephone surveys or written surveys.

2. **Treat your customers by using the personal touch.** When you converse with your customers by telephone, indicate your willingness to listen to their needs anytime. Write letters to them that thank them for their business.

3. **Add your customers' names to mailing lists for publications or newsletters that your company publishes, if there are any.** Customers who have received quality customer service generally like to learn of new products and services, updates, and changes occurring within your company.

4. **Reward and recognize customers for their business and interest.** For example, if a customer refers a possible new customer to your company, let the customer know you appreciate the referral. You can show your appreciation by writing or calling the customer.

5. **Offer special discounts or other similar programs to promote goodwill with your customers.** You will reward your customers for their past business and increase the chances for future business.

6. **Provide standards of excellence for all employees who deal with customers.** Procedures for managing certain customer service requests and concerns should be established and understood by all customer service representatives. These standards and expectations indicate that your business is committed to top customer service performance.

7. **Ask for suggestions from all customers.** The best ideas for improvement often come from customers. Get their input regularly.

8. **Be willing to negotiate possible solutions that will keep everyone satisfied.** This willingness will lead to increased customer satisfaction.

9. **Recognize that problems will occur with products and service.** Be ready to work through them in a positive manner when they arise.

10. **Know your customers so that you will be able to offer the best possible service to them.** Become familiar with customers' preferences, dislikes, and product or service goals. They will remember your concern and kindness.

Summary

1. Positive customer service is important in establishing goodwill in any business. The lack of positive customer service can result in loss of clients and business, sometimes permanently.

2. Everyone with whom you come in contact is a potential customer. Provide services that will meet the customers' needs positively and invite them to continue doing business with you.

3. You must provide quality customer service in order to keep your customers.

4. When you talk on the telephone, your voice is very important in providing and receiving quality customer service.

5. Your voice is what the recipient "hears." Remember to smile when talking on the telephone. It makes your voice sound pleasant.

6. Special challenges can be presented when you want to reach a specific person in a customer service call.

7. Answer the telephone on the first or second ring. If the phone continues to ring, the caller will not appreciate your lateness and could feel neglected.

8. Active listening is important to communicating effectively with customers.

9. Ask the right questions to carry out customer service effectively.

10. Answering devices, such as voice mail, answering machines, and pagers, are important in telephone technology today.

11. Customer service professionals recognize that placing a message on voice mail or an answering machine can create a gap between them and their customers. Because of this gap, the possibility exists that the customer and the professional may never be in touch with each other again.

12. Expert customer service centers around questions. The questions should help you provide service for your customers with a personal, helpful style.

13. Answering devices can increase productivity and serve customers better if customer service representatives return calls to customers who have left messages.

14. Pagers, or beepers, can improve customer service because they instantly notify the user of a call. This is especially important when the user is unreachable by phone.

15. The Internet, e-mail, and the World Wide Web are being used more and more to purchase many products and services. These technologies also are being used to report and respond to customer service needs.

16. When a customer raises an objection, you must handle the situation quickly and effectively.

17. Listening is the key to managing objections.

Reinforcement Application 7

Your Perception of Customer Service

Directions: On the lines provided below, list several major reasons why customers might want to discontinue doing business with a company. Then, for each of these reasons, write suggestions for correcting the poor customer service. Be specific and ready to justify your answers.

Reasons for Discontinuing Business	Suggestions for Correcting Poor Customer Service
1.	
2.	
3.	
4.	
5.	
6.	
7.	
8.	
9.	
10.	

Case Study 5

Assessing Customer Service

Directions: Analyze the situation described below and then answer the questions that follow. Try to provide answers that reflect your understanding of the concepts presented in Chapter 5.

Clothing Unlimited Company is very successful. You have recently accepted a position as the customer service manager and are anxious to keep the reputation of the company at a high level. In order to gather feedback from customers, you decide to conduct a telephone survey to 100 customers over the next two months.

The survey yields this interesting information:

- 55 percent rated customer service as "average"
- 25 percent rated customer service as "poor"
- 15 percent rated customer service as "good"
- 5 percent rated customer service as "outstanding"

1. Does the fact that only 5 percent indicated customer service was outstanding mean anything? If so, what?

_____

_____

_____

_____

_____

_____

2. What do you feel will happen to Clothing Unlimited Company if this situation is not corrected?

_____

_____

_____

_____

_____

_____

3. List at least three major considerations that Clothing Unlimited Company should consider implementing in order to upgrade its overall customer service.

_____

_____

_____

_____

_____

_____

4. Do you feel this telephone survey was effective? Why or why not?

_____

_____

_____

_____

_____

_____

5. What unique factors might be considered in a telephone survey conducted about Clothing Unlimited Company?

_____

_____

_____

_____

_____

_____

Using Telephone Equipment and Technology

OBJECTIVES

Chapter 6 will help you:

1. Understand the role of telephone equipment and technology in the communication process.

2. Develop a working knowledge of the telephone equipment and technology available.

3. Evaluate today's telephone equipment and technology in order to make wise decisions regarding equipment and technology for the workplace.

TODAY'S TELEPHONE TECHNOLOGY

Alexander Graham Bell's experimentation and research led to the ultimate invention of the telephone in 1876. The early beginnings of telephone technology were centered totally around equipment because of the need to make connections between phones. The progress in telephone equipment development and technology today is an outgrowth of this work.

The telephone is not the only piece of equipment used in the telephone communication process. Many pieces of telephone-related or auxiliary equipment are used to help make the process of communication faster and more convenient, wherever the location. Telephone equipment that is properly installed and used can provide a fast line of communication to the entire world at any time, at the touch of the fingers.

TELEPHONES

The need for telephones and appropriate equipment should be a high priority for you and your company. Select a telephone system that enables and enhances your communication needs.

Selection

Before shopping for telephone equipment, ask yourself these questions:

1. What is the size of the business?
2. Where will the business be located?
3. How many telephones will meet your needs?
4. How many telephone lines will meet your needs?
5. What other auxiliary equipment or technology should you consider?
6. Should you purchase, rent, or lease the equipment?

Be sure the telephone system you choose is easy to use in serving people inside and outside your company.

Chapter 1 stressed that "You never get a second chance to make a good first impression." This is especially true when communicating with people over the telephone. Evaluate a telephone system carefully. Be sure it is easy to use in serving your customers, potential customers, coworkers, and everyone with whom you do business.

Consider these options when purchasing telephone equipment and services. Refer to Chapter 3 for detailed information on these items.

- An effective answering service with voice-mail capabilities
- Call forwarding
- Call waiting
- Conference calling

Depending on the size of your business, you may also want to consider the need for video conferencing. Video conferencing equipment allows a business to communicate visually with another business. The businesses can be in different cities around the world; however, both sites must have equipment that is compatible.

Some businesses offer a toll-free telephone number for incoming calls. Callers may use the number at no charge. The business pays a flat rate for all of the toll-free calls. Having a toll-free number promotes goodwill to customers and potential customers. In addition, the toll-free number may save the business money, depending on the number of calls.

Whether you buy one telephone or many, you need to consider what will best meet your business needs when choosing telephone equipment. The telephones must function well for your business, and they should also be durable enough to withstand much use. Telephones are available in a variety of styles, options, and other personalized features. Check your local *Yellow Pages* for suppliers and telephone manufacturers near you.

Figure 6-1 Telephones are available with various styles, options, and features.

Cordless Telephones

A *cordless telephone*, often called a portable phone, operates by using a transmitter and a receiver in both the headset and the base. Cordless phones are popular because they are portable and available in many styles and features. (See Figure 6-2.)

The headset of a cordless phone uses batteries. The base of the phone must be connected to a telephone line and plugged into an electrical outlet. A cordless phone operates over selected channels, which can cause interference and security problems. Although a cordless phone is portable, it works only within a certain range. For example, the headset must be within 100 feet from the base.

Figure 6-2 Cordless phones are portable and are available with various styles and features.

Cellular Telephones

Cellular phones, which also are portable, may be referred to as car phones, portable phones, or even mobile phones. (See Figure 6-3.) Unlike cordless phones, however, you can use cellular phones virtually anywhere.

A cellular phone operates basically like a two-way radio. Some models for use in cars must be plugged into the cigarette lighter or require batteries to operate. When shopping for a cellular phone, be sure you evaluate the battery to determine its capacity for receiving and transmitting calls.

Evaluate the capacity of a cellular phone battery before you make a decision to purchase a cellular phone.

Evaluate promotions offered by cellular phone carriers. These offers can add hidden costs to the cost of your phone.

If your cellular phone will be used in the car, choose features that will allow you to keep both hands on the steering wheel while using the phone. Select a phone that is lightweight and convenient in size.

Cellular phone service is provided by licensed cellular phone carriers. These carriers are regulated by the Federal Communications Commission. Choose a service agreement and phone that best suit your needs. Evaluate free promotions that some carriers may offer. Often the promotions may have hidden costs that can add a lot to the cost of your phone. Shop wisely for any cellular phone, no matter where it will be used.

Figure 6-3 Cellular phones can be used virtually anywhere.

Some negative factors should be recognized when using a cellular phone. You may experience reception interference resulting from topography, such as hills or trees, and electrical towers. Poor weather, like thunderstorms, also may cause interference and pose a safety hazard when using a cellular phone.

Equipment for Special Needs

Many products are available to help people who have vision, motion, speech, or hearing losses or impairments use the telephone.

To aid the person with impaired or loss of vision, some telephones have special features for the keypad. These features include oversized numbers, an enlarged touch-tone keypad, or can be purchased that use a raised touch-tone keypad. Stickers of enlarged numbers may be placed on the keypad of regular touch-tone phones. An insert with enlarged numbers may be used on rotary-dial telephones.

The raised and enlarged touch-tone keypad can assist a user who experiences motion loss or impairment in pressing the correct buttons. An overlay for the keypad is also available that can automatically dial the operator when it is pressed. A device also enables a breath of air to place, receive, and disconnect calls.

To aid the deaf and hard of hearing, the TTY devices (Text Telephone Yoke), sometimes referred to as TDD, or telecommunications devices for the deaf, are used to type telephone messages. The messages are sent over telephone lines and printed at a receiving TTY. Fax machines also may be used to send and receive messages. In addition, computers can be used for communicating by on-line services and electronic mail.

Persons with speech loss or impairment may use an artificial larynx (voice box) to produce sounds for speaking on the telephone. Other devices attach to the telephone to amplify weak voices. Persons with speech loss or impairment also may use a TTY.

AUXILIARY TELEPHONE EQUIPMENT

Auxiliary equipment for the telephone is used to enable and enhance communication. For example, answering machines can record messages for an unanswered phone. Fax machines can provide written confirmation of items discussed over the phone.

Answering Machines

Figure 6-4 Some answering machines use a tape to record messages; some record messages digitally.

Answering machines are available with many setups and features. Some models must be connected to the telephone, and others are stand-alone machines. Some models record messages using a cassette tape, and others record digitally. Check your telephone owner's manual to know the type of answering machine your telephone can accommodate.

Modems

Modem is a short term for modulator/demodulator. A modem is an electronic device used to send data from one computer to another across telephone lines. The device converts electronic data and images from a sending computer into signals for the receiving computer. The receiving computer, in turn, converts the signals into a form that it can understand.

Modems are available as separate devices; however, they are more commonly built into computers.

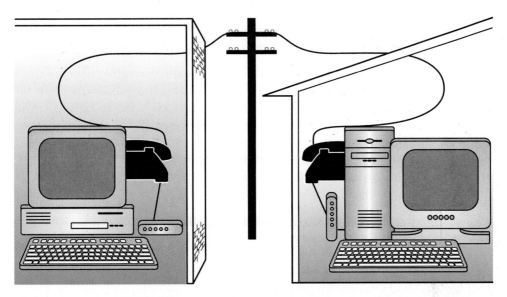

Figure 6-5 A modem enables data to be transmitted between computers across telephone lines.

Consider these points when selecting a modem.

1. **Speed.** A modem's speed is measured by its baud rate. The baud rate is the speed at which the modem converts signals. The higher the baud rate, the faster the modem operates.

2. **Hayes-compatibility**. Hayes-compatibility is the common modem language used by most computers today. This means that usually the modem will support most software.

3. **Software needs.** The modem you purchase should come with software that will meet your needs. For example, the modem should allow you to use electronic-mail features and certain on-line services.

Facsimile Machines

A *fax machine* (facsimile machine) can electronically read, send, and receive characters and most forms of graphics that are transmitted over a telephone line. A telephone is part of, or is connected to, a fax machine.

A telephone line is necessary to send and receive faxes. The line may be the regular phone line or a separate telephone line dedicated for this purpose. The decision to install a dedicated line usually depends on how much the line will be used and the size of the business. Consider these advantages of having a dedicated telephone line for faxing:

- The line will always be available for immediate use.

- Messages can be received and transmitted 24 hours a day.
- Use of the telephone will not interfere with use of the fax machine.

A fax machine, or device, may be a stand-alone device. It can also be part of a computer. Ask your manufacturer or supplier about the advantages and disadvantages of each type.

At the sending, or transmitting, fax machine, the operator inserts a document into the fax machine feed tray. The operator then dials the destination fax machine. When the telephone connection is made between the two machines, the sending fax machine scans, or sends, the document that is inserted. The document can include words, graphics, photographs, and even signatures. At the destination fax machine, the call is answered, or accepted. Then the message being sent is printed on blank paper that is inserted in the machine.

The speed of transmission and reception varies, depending on the density of the text in the document being sent and the fax machine. Usually several pages may be sent each minute. The clarity of a faxed document containing text—and especially graphics, photographs, and signatures—will be less than that of the original document.

Several factors must be considered when purchasing a fax machine.

1. **Cost and the quality of the transmission.** Fax machines receive messages on either thermal paper or plain paper. Thermal-paper fax machines cost less than plain-paper fax machines. Plain-paper fax machines produce higher quality documents.

2. **Options.** Options include copying capabilities, redial, adjustments for contrast and resolution, and memory, to name a few. Study the literature from fax machine manufacturers to help you choose the right machine.

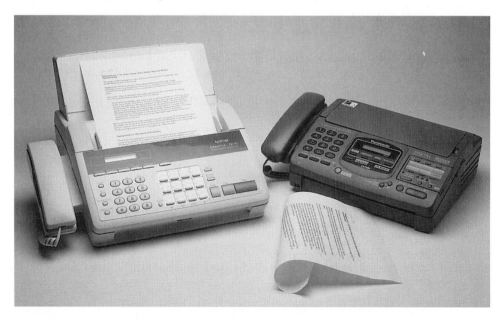

Figure 6-6 Fax machines receive documents on either plain paper or thermal paper.

(I) GLOBAL Commerce
603 Berkshire
Omaha, NE 68127
402-555-0987

Date: _____
Fax To: _____
Company: _____
Fax No: _____

From: Fax:
Subject: No. of Pages:

MESSAGE:

_____
_____
_____
_____
_____
_____
_____
_____
_____

Figure 6-7 A fax cover sheet.

FAX TIPS

You should reflect a professional image when using the telephone. Likewise, reflect a professional image with the materials you send by a facsimile machine. The documents should be neat and include all important information.

1. **Include a fax cover sheet, or transmittal sheet.** (See the example shown in Figure 6-7.)

   A fax cover sheet should contain these items:

   - Date
   - Sender's name
   - Sender's company name and address
   - Sender's telephone number
   - Sender's fax number
   - Sender's e-mail address, if available
   - Number of pages being sent
   - Recipient's name
   - Recipient's company name
   - Recipient's fax number
   - Space for a brief transmittal message

Preprinted fax cover sheets are available at most office supply centers.

2. **Limit fax transmissions to as few pages as possible.** If you have numerous pages to send, consider sending them by another method, such as overnight delivery or mail. Be concise in fax documents.

3. **Use fonts (typefaces) in your document that are easily readable.** Most fax machines receive documents in reduced size, so choose fonts carefully. Use simple, plain fonts, rather than decorative or elaborate fonts (e.g., wide, thick, or script characters). Also, use 12 point size or larger fonts. Avoid using numerous fonts, which can confuse the reader and distract from the message.

Pagers

Choose a pager with a display that you can easily read.

Pagers and beepers are widely used and have several options. Choose a pager that is of a convenient size and is not cumbersome. Check the display to be sure you can easily read it. Purchase a pager with features that you will use; unused features will cost you money.

ACTIVITY 28: Selecting Telephones

The purpose of this activity is to help you understand the importance of properly assessing and selecting telephones.

Select two people to interview concerning their preferences on the purchase of telephones. Use the questions below as guidelines, and ask other appropriate questions that arise during the interview. Share your findings with the class.

1. How many telephones do you use either personally or professionally?

2. What were your considerations when you purchased your phone(s)?

3. Are the telephones adequately meeting your needs? If not, why not?

4. What other types of auxiliary telephone equipment and technology might you consider useful for your needs? Why or why not?

5. What other recommendations do you have for purchasing telephones and auxiliary telephone equipment?

The purpose of this activity is to help you properly assess auxiliary telephone equipment. The person described in each scenario below is using auxiliary telephone equipment in order to be more efficient. Read each statement and then indicate the equipment that applies best, choosing from the letters a through e for your responses.

    a. Answering machine

    b. Voice Mail

    c. Pager

    d. Modem

    e. Fax machine

_____ 1. When Kenneth Dearborn arrived at work this morning, he noticed the red light flashing on his telephone, indicating that he had messages.

_____ 2. Ryan Randall used this device to transmit electronic data from his company's computer to his client's computer.

_____ 3. Allyn Hutton called her office when this device sounded a tone.

_____ 4. Gabriella Dubois needs to send a two-page schedule concerning upcoming meetings to another colleague in her state.

_____ 5. Joshua Borden called a company to speak with a sales associate concerning a special order. The sales associate is not in but would like to have Joshua leave a message.

ON-LINE TECHNOLOGY

On-line technology uses computers and telephone lines or electronic devices to transmit and receive data. This technology already provides many products and services to individuals and businesses. In addition, the relationship between computers and telephones will continue to provide more opportunities as businesses and services expand globally.

The on-line services used most frequently include electronic mail (or e-mail) and the Internet. You will recall these terms from Chapter 5.

Electronic Mail (E-Mail)

Electronic mail, also referred to as *e-mail*, is a means of sharing information or communicating between users by way of electronic messages. To communicate by e-mail, you must subscribe to an e-mail service. E-mail services are available through many on-line service providers. Many providers connect service via a telephone line. Subscription prices for e-mail service vary.

E-mail communication is sent from and received at an e-mail address. An e-mail address may contain an abbreviated part of the company or individual's name, an abbreviated part of the on-line service provider's name, and other parts, known as subdomains and domains. For example, an e-mail address might read:

janedoe@doestore.com

jdoe@aol.gov

jdoe@education.mci.net

Some of the advantages of using e-mail are:

- **It can save money.** Messages can be written off-line before they are sent on-line.

- **It can be sent at your convenience.** Time zone differences do not affect sending e-mail messages.

- **It can be read at your convenience.** You can eliminate telephone tag and the need to make repeat calls.

- **It can notify the sender that a recipient has opened an e-mail message.** You can eliminate placing repeat calls and leaving messages.

Be prepared to follow up e-mail messages that are not answered within a reasonable amount of time. You may want to phone or send another message to that person.

E-mail is similar to regular mail in some ways. It must be opened, like a letter in an envelope. Just because it was opened, however, does not mean it has been read by the recipient. If you do not receive a return e-mail or other type of message within a reasonable amount of time, be prepared to follow up. Consider making a telephone call or sending another e-mail message.

MANAGING E-MAIL MESSAGES

Use these guidelines to help you manage your e-mail professionally.

1. **Check your e-mail daily.** Messages can be sent anytime. Check periodically to avoid missing important messages. Some messages may require timely action or follow up.

2. **Delete unnecessary messages; save important ones.** After you have read your e-mail, delete messages that need no reply. Keep messages that you must respond to or follow up.

3. **Be aware that e-mail can be monitored.** Some businesses monitor e-mail for security reasons. Be careful what you send and to whom you send it.

4. **Be professional in all e-mail correspondence.** Use the same courtesies as you would if the message were in hard copy, such as a letter or memo.

5. **Be concise.** Avoid using unnecessary words. Keep your message brief.

6. **Use a memo format for messages.** It is not necessary to format an e-mail message in a letter format—the simpler the better.

7. **Avoid shouting.** E-mail users should respect e-mail etiquette. The use of all-capital letters in messages is considered equal to verbally shouting. The use of all-capital letters can dilute the real message.

8. **Proofread messages before sending them.** As with all correspondence, review and proofread e-mail messages before sending them.

The Internet

The *Internet* is a worldwide collection of computer networks. The networks are electronically connected to permit communication and the exchange of information. Databases, libraries, and other information sources are available for thousands of topics ranging from simple to complex.

You must subscribe to an Internet service to use the Internet. This service is available through several on-line service providers. Most providers connect service to the Internet via a telephone line and a modem. Subscription prices for Internet service vary.

An important part of the Internet is the World Wide Web, also known as *The Web* or *WWW*. The Web is a place on the Internet where documents and information are stored for use. Web pages use graphics and text to show information about topics.

ACTIVITY 30: Choosing Auxiliary Telephone Equipment and Tools

The purpose of this activity is to learn to properly assess and choose between auxiliary telephone equipment and tools. Read each scenario below. Then indicate which auxiliary telephone device(s) or tools would best suit each situation. Be prepared to justify your answer.

1. You need to send a one-page letter instead of making a telephone call.

   _____

2. You are in the attic searching for tax records in preparation for going to your accountant. You want to be able to answer any calls.

   _____

3. You are traveling 350 miles on business and want to have a telephone available for your use during your travel.

   _____

4. You will be away from your desk for two days but wish to receive all your calls.

   _____

5. You want to be able to receive any messages immediately wherever you are.

   _____

6. You would like to be able to do some shopping in the convenience of your home via a computer.

   _____

7. You want to be able to communicate electronically with your staff located at ten places in the United States.

   _____

THE TELEPHONE AS A MAJOR TOOL FOR THE FUTURE

The telephone will play a major role in the communication process for the next several years. Each year the telephone and other technologies will continue to expand. New telephones and auxiliary telephone-related equipment will be developed in order to meet customer needs.

We often forget how important the telephone is in our daily lives and business affairs. Yet, tomorrow the telephone will remain central to us. It will be further adapted to enable and complement many other communication technologies.

Summary

1. Alexander Graham Bell's research and work led to the invention of the telephone in 1876. For some time after, telephone technology focused on developing equipment because of the need to make connections between phones. The progress in telephone equipment and technology today is an outgrowth of this work.

2. Telephone equipment that is properly installed and used can provide a fast line of communication to the entire world, at any time, at the touch of the fingers.

3. The need for telephones and equipment should be a high priority for you and your company.

4. Evaluate a telephone system carefully. Be sure it will adequately serve your customers, potential customers, coworkers, and everyone with whom you do business.

5. When choosing telephone equipment, think what will best meet your needs, whether you buy one telephone or many.

6. Cordless phones are popular because they are portable and available in many styles and features.

7. Cellular phones may be referred to as car phones, portable phones, or even mobile phones. Unlike cordless phones, however, you can use cellular phones virtually anywhere.

8. Many products are available to help people with vision, motion, speech, or hearing losses or impairments use the telephone.

9. A modem is an electronic device used to send data from one computer to another across telephone lines.

10. A fax machine (facsimile machine) can electronically read, send, and receive characters and most forms of illustration transmitted over a telephone line.

11. Pagers and beepers are widely used and have several options.

12. On-line technology uses computers and telephone lines or electronic devices to transmit and receive data. This technology already provides many products and services to individuals and businesses. The on-line services used most frequently include electronic mail (or e-mail) and the Internet.

Reinforcement Application 8

Recommending Telephone and Auxiliary Equipment

Directions: Assume that Natasha Winslow is opening her own small business, where she will manage all the calls. On the lines provided below, write a statement recommending the type of telephone and auxiliary telephone equipment Natasha should purchase. Base your recommendations on what you have studied in Chapter 6. Report this information to your classmates or as your instructor directs you.

_____

_____

_____

_____

_____

_____

_____

_____

_____

_____

_____

_____

Case Study 6

The Home Insurance Adjuster

Directions: Analyze the situation described below and then answer the questions that follow. Try to provide answers that reflect your understanding of the concepts presented in Chapter 6.

Cherise Nguben is an insurance adjuster for a large insurance company that processes claims electronically. In her job, Cherise uses the telephone continuously. She also receives calls from claims adjusters in the field, who are difficult to reach because they frequently travel. Cherise uses e-mail and her fax machine to send documents and data electronically in communicating with coworkers (both in her building and at other branch offices) and clients.

The company has agreed to Cherise's request to work out of her home. In order to facilitate her work, it will provide for Cherise a computer and any necessary auxiliary telephone equipment.

1. What type of telephone would best serve Cherise's needs? Why?

   _____

   _____

   _____

   _____

2. Would a cordless phone or a cellular phone be useful to Cherise? Why or why not?

   _____

   _____

   _____

   _____

3. What auxiliary telephone equipment will Cherise need? Why?

   _____

   _____

   _____

   _____

4. What additional telephone services, features, or equipment would be useful to Cherise for:

   a. Ensuring that she misses no calls?

   _____

   _____

   _____

   _____

   b. Covering the telephone when she is unavailable?

   _____

   _____

   _____

   _____

   c. Quickly dialing outgoing calls?

   _____

   _____

   _____

   _____

Glossary

A

additional listing: A service with which several people having the same phone number may each have a separate listing in the directory.

air phone: A type of cellular telephone available for use in airplanes.

answering machine: A machine that answers phone calls and records messages if someone does not answer the phone.

appointment calendar: A calendar that lists days, weeks, or months; may also list times or include blank space with each day, week, or month for recording appointments; available in printed or electronic format.

appointment scheduling call: A telephone call in which an appointment is scheduled.

area code: A three-digit number that identifies each unique telephone service area in a country (such as the United States or Canada).

artificial larynx: Artificial voice box; can be used to produce sounds for speaking on the telephone.

automated attendant: A machine or recording that directs callers to an appropriate party or department by way of a series of instructions.

automatic callback: Repeat dialing; a service that redials the last number called when that line is no longer busy.

auxiliary telephone equipment: Telephone-related equipment that is used to enable and enhance the communication process. Examples are pagers, answering machines, and facsimile machines.

B

background question: A question that helps you direct a caller to the correct department or person or obtain important information in order to serve the customer.

baud rate: The speed at which a modem converts signals; the higher the baud rate, the faster a modem operates.

beeper: *See* pager.

business listings: Entries of businesses and organizations in a telephone directory.

busy call forwarding: A service that transfers incoming calls automatically when the line called is busy.

C

call blocking: A service that eliminates the display of your number on any caller ID display device or panel.

call forwarding: A service that allows you to transfer incoming calls to another number.

call pickup: A service that enables an incoming call to be accessed on any telephone within a system (such as within a company); the user must enter a code to pick up the call.

call trace: A service that determines the source of the most recent incoming call.

call waiting: A service that alerts you of an incoming call by sounding a quiet beeping tone during the current call.

caller ID: A service that displays the number of an incoming call on a special panel or device.

calling card: A card, which looks similar to a credit card, that is assigned to an individual or a telephone number. With this card, you can make calls of many types from almost any location in the United States without coins and little or no operator assistance. This card is provided by most major long-distance telephone companies.

cellular telephone: A mobile telephone that is often used in vehicles, planes, boats, and elsewhere. The user can make and receive telephone calls on this phone.

closed question: A question that can be answered with *yes* or *no*; used to verify information; often starts with *are you, do you, can, could, did, will,* and *would.*

collect call: A telephone call in which the person called agrees to pay the charges for the call.

collection call: A telephone call in which the goal of the caller is to collect money for an account balance by getting a commitment from the recipient to pay.

colloquial expression: A word or phrase characteristic of informal conversation, such as *bye-bye* or *see yah*. Such expressions should be avoided in professional telephone conversations.

communication: The process of exchanging ideas and messages either verbally or nonverbally; consists of four major parts: speaking, reading, writing, and listening.

company directory: A directory of telephone numbers and internal extensions that is published by a company to make internal communication easier and more efficient; formats include electronic lists or databases or hard copies in looseleaf binders.

complaint call: A telephone call in which a person complains about a mistake in a product or service.

conclusion: The final stage of a telephone call in which the caller and receiver come to an understanding of the action to be taken by each of them and then say good-bye.

conference call: A telephone call that permits three or more parties to communicate on a single call; can be any combination of local or long-distance calls.

cordless telephone: A portable telephone that operates by a transmitter and a receiver in both the headset and the base.

courtesy: Polite and considerate behavior when communicating with people on the telephone; one of the bench marks of positive telephone skills.

customer service: The management and follow-up of questions, concerns, and complaints regarding products and/or services.

customer service professional: Customer service representative; one who manages customer service telephone calls.

D

dedicated telephone line: A telephone line used solely for sending and receiving faxes or for a purpose other than making and receiving telephone calls.

delayed call forwarding: A service that transfers calls automatically if the phone is not answered within a specified number of rings.

directory assistance: A service that provides access to many telephone numbers and/or addresses.

disconnected call: A call that is disconnected, or terminated; may be caused by accidentally pressing a button that terminates the call, by storms, overloaded circuits, or power failures.

discreet: To be careful not to reveal any inappropriate information.

distraction: Noise, action, or sound that distracts from a telephone conversation.

E

e-mail: *See* electronic mail.

electronic mail: E-mail; a means of sharing information or communicating between users by way of electronic messages.

enunciation: The clarity with which you speak.

ergonomic: A design or arrangement of office equipment, materials, fixtures, and lighting in a way that promotes effective, safe interaction between the people using the items and the items themselves.

evaluating: The third stage of listening that forces you to think about the whole message and make conclusions about the content and the way in which you will respond.

extension: A two-, three-, or four-digit number assigned to a phone within a company's telephone network.

F

facsimile machine: Fax machines; a machine that can electronically read, send, and receive characters and most forms of illustration transmitted over a telephone line.

fax machine: *See* facsimile machine.

fax transmittal sheet: A cover sheet preceding a faxed document that includes information about the sender and receiver, including: date, sender's name, sender's company name, sender's company address, sender's telephone number, sender's fax number, sender's e-mail address, number of pages being sent, recipient's name, recipient's company name, recipient's fax number, and space for a brief transmittal message.

font: Typeface or style of type used in a word processed document.

forced-choice question: A question that requires an "either-or" response and gives the listener two or more options from which to select.

H

Hayes-compatibility: The common modem language used by most computers.

headset: An attachment that holds an earphone and transmitter on one's head; also the portion of a cordless telephone which you hold in your hand that contains a hearing and speaking device.

hold: To delay temporarily the managing of a telephone call so that information can be obtained, the recipient can speak to another person, or another call can be answered or managed.

I

individual call transfer: A service that enables a user to transfer a call to another phone without an operator's help.

information request call: A telephone call that involves the exchanging of information ranging from simple to complex.

international call: A long-distance telephone call made to a location in another country.

international city code: A number, or code, used in an international telephone call to access a specific city of a specific country.

international country code: A number, or code, used in an international telephone call to access a specific country.

Internet: A worldwide collection of computer networks; the networks are electronically connected to permit communication and the exchange of information; databases, libraries, and other information sources are available for thousands of topics.

interpreting: The second stage in listening in which you identify what is said and interpret the speaker's meaning.

interruption: An action that forces a break in a telephone conversation and redirects your attention from the call to another party.

introduction: The first stage of a telephone call in which both parties identify themselves and the caller establishes the convenience of the call.

L

listening: The act of hearing someone's words and thoughts, and then responding.

listening roadblock: Any interference to effective listening during a telephone call, such as a distraction, an interruption, or a disconnected call.

local call: A telephone call made to a location within the local calling area; this type of call may be billed per call, based on the length of the call; often billed at a flat monthly fee.

logging: The process of keeping track of calls.

long-distance call: A telephone call that is made to a location outside of the local calling area; billed separately from local calls; rates are based on the call's destination, day of the week, time of day, length of the conversation, and any operator services requested.

M

modem: A short term for modulator/demodulator; an electronic device that sends data from one computer to another across telephone lines by converting electronic data and images from a sending computer into signals for the receiving computer; available as a separate device and built into a computer.

N

nondirectory listed number: A service with which your telephone number will not appear in the telephone directory but will be available from directory assistance.

nonpublished number: A service with which your telephone number will not appear in the telephone directory and will not be released by directory assistance.

O

objection: Disagreement or disapproval presented with a suggestion, comment, or proposed benefit or idea.

on-line technology: The use of computers and telephone lines or electronic devices to transmit and receive data.

open question: A type of question that requires a *yes* or *no* answer; usually begin with *who, what, where, when, why,* and *how.*

overlay: An item for the telephone keypad that automatically dials the operator when it is pressed; the operator then assists the person with making the call.

P

pager: Beeper; a small, portable device that notifies the wearer of an incoming call via a beeping tone or vibration.

person-to-person call: A telephone call that allows the caller to speak only with a specific person (in some cases, an extension) by way of operator assistance.

personal directory: A person's record of frequently called telephone numbers; common formats are an electronic list or database, a book with alphabetical listings, or a rotary file.

phone-number-only: A service that allows you to list your name and home number and just a portion or none of your address in the telephone directory.

pitch: The variation in highness or lowness of your voice.

plain-paper fax: A facsimile machine that uses plain paper for receiving faxed documents.

point size: Size of a font or typeface.

prepaid phone card: A card, similar to a calling card, that allows the user to make telephone calls without coins, except the charges are paid for in advance; usually an access code or number must be dialed to begin the call. These cards are available from many sources and in various allotments of time and dollar amounts.

productivity: The state or quality of being productive, or supplying results, profits, or benefits.

professional: Characteristic of proper business conduct and communication; a manner of communicating that creates a sense of satisfac-

tion for both parties. Also, one who represents a company in communicating by way of the telephone.

pronunciation: The correct way to say a word.

purpose: The second stage of a telephone call in which the caller communicates his or her needs clearly; the caller must also understand the other person's needs in relation to the purpose of the call.

R

redial: A function or service available on some telephones that dials the last number called again when a special key is pressed or a code is entered.

residence listings: Entries of community residents in a telephone directory.

responding: The fourth stage of listening that requires you to make a statement verbally.

S

screen: To monitor incoming calls prior to forwarding them to another person; after the recipient identifies himself or herself and the company, the caller must identify himself or herself and the purpose of the call; used to determine whether or not to forward a call to a manager or other employee.

selective call waiting: A service with which you can temporarily cancel the call-waiting tone so that it will not interrupt the current conversation.

sensing: The first stage in listening in which you are aware that someone is saying something to which you need to listen; if it does not occur, the listening process never begins.

slang: Informal vocabulary consisting of arbitrarily changed words, or fancy, forced, or witty figures of speech; sometimes considered harsh or coarse language.

speed calling: A service that allows you to dial frequently called local and long-distance numbers automatically.

switchboard: A central or controlling telephone for a business, usually monitored by a receptionist or switchboard operator; all incoming calls may be received at the switchboard and then routed to the appropriate person or department.

T

tact: A smart sense of what to say or do in order to maintain goodwill and professionalism.

TDD: See TTY.

telemarketer: A person trained on the product or service being marketed by way of the telephone; must have excellent oral communication skills, quick decision-making abilities, and strong listening skills; must reflect a positive attitude, have a pleasant voice, and be persistent but not overly aggressive.

telemarketing: The process of using the telephone to market or sell a product or service.

telephone directory: A book that lists telephone numbers of residences and businesses and other reference information.

telephone tag: A situation in which two parties return calls to each other but never make contact with one another.

TeleTYpe: See TTY.

Text Telephone Yoke: a device or machine for typing telephone messages used by persons with speech loss, speech impairment, deafness, or those who are hard of hearing; messages are sent over telephone lines, and printed at a receiving TTY machine. Also referred to as TeleTYpe machine or TDD, telecommunications devices for the deaf.

The Web: See World Wide Web.

thermal-paper fax: A facsimile machine that uses thermal paper for receiving faxed documents.

third-number billing: A service that bills a long-distance call to a phone besides the one you are calling to or from.

time zone: A geographical region of time.

toll-free telephone number: A number offered by a business for callers to use without charge; usually begins with an 800 prefix in place of an area code.

tone: Style or manner of expression that conveys your attitude in speaking.

touch-tone service: A service that makes the dialing process easier and quicker and assigns a specific tone to each number and symbol on the telephone keypad; must be used to complete many "computer-assisted" calls that require options to be selected using buttons on the phone.

transfer: To reroute a telephone call to another person or department that is better equipped or able to help the caller.

TTY: See Text Telephone Yoke.

two-person directory listing: A service that allows two people with the same last name living at the same address to list both of their first names in the telephone directory at no charge.

V

verification question: Confirmation question; a type of question that verifies or confirms that information provided is correct or understood.

video conferencing equipment: Equipment that allows a business to communicate visually with another business; the businesses can be in different cities around the world; both sites must have equipment that is compatible.

voice mail: An automated system used to record incoming telephone messages, usually subscribed to through a telephone service or company.

voice quality: The way you speak over the telephone that creates a picture of yourself in the mind of the person at the other end of the telephone conversation; includes the pitch, tone, and speed of your voice.

W

White Pages: A local telephone directory that provides an alphabetic listing of names and telephone numbers and other telephone reference information.

World Wide Web: The Web or WWW; a place on the Internet where documents and information are stored for use; Web pages use graphics and text to show information about topics.

WWW: See World Wide Web.

Y

Yellow Pages: A local directory of listings or display ads for organizations and businesses arranged alphabetically by subject heading; the listings are often cross-referenced under related headings; can appear within the telephone directory, or may be published separately.

Index

A

Accent, 5
Active listening, 9
Additional listing, 70
Answering machines, 29
Appointment scheduling call, 86–87
Attitude, 10
Automated attendant, 30
Automatic callback, 71
Auxiliary telephone equipment, 128–132
   answering machines, 128
   fax (facsimile) machines, 129–132
   modems, 128–129

B

Beepers (*see* pagers)

C

Calendar, 86
Call blocking, 71
Call forwarding, 70
Call pickup, 71
Call trace, 71
Call waiting, 70
Caller ID, 71
Callers on hold, 16, 38–39
Calling cards, 68
Car phones, 126
Cellular telephones, 126–127
Collect calls, 65
Collection calls, 94–95
Communication, 3
Complaint calls, 90–94
   making, 90–91
   responding to, 93–94
Concluding calls, 22–23
Conference calls, 68, 71
Cordless telephones, 125–126
Costs of calling, 72–73
Customer service
   answering techniques, 109
   asking questions, 110
   listening, 110–111
   objections, 117
   professionals, 104
   proper identification, 107–108
   quality, 104
   representatives, 104
   tips, 117–118
   understanding customer needs, 116–117
   voice, 5–7, 104–106

D

Delayed call forwarding, 70
Dialect, 5
Directories, 29, 59–63
Directory assistance, 64
Directory listing, 68, 70
   additional listing, 70
   nondirectory listed number, 70
   nonpublished number, 70
   phone-number only, 68
   two-person listing, 68
Disconnected calls, 11, 13
Discreet, 35
Distractions, 12

E

E-mail addresses, 29
Enunciation, 5
Equipment for special needs, 127–128
   artificial larynx, 127
   keypad, 127
   TDD, 127–128
   TTY, 127–128
Extensions, 29, 63

F

Facsimile cover sheet, 131–132
Facsimile (fax) machines, 129–130
Fax numbers, 29

H

Hold, putting calls on, 16, 38–39

I

Incoming calls, 29, 31–32
   answering and managing, 31
   identifying yourself, 31–32
   routing, 29
Individual call transfer, 71
Information call, 81–82, 85–86
   obtaining information, 81–82
   providing information, 85–86
International calls, 63–64
Interruptions, 11–12
Introduction, 16

L

Listening, 7–10, 14–15
Logging (recording) calls, 42–43
Long-distance calls, 17, 73

M

Making telephone calls, 55–57, 63–64
   collection calls, 94–95
   complaint calls, 90–94
   international, 63–64
   locating numbers for, 29, 59, 81
   scheduling, 57
   telemarketing, 95–98
   telephone readiness, 55
Marine calls, 66
Messages, taking, 43–45
Mobile calls, 66
Modems, 128–129

N

Nondirectory listed number, 70
Nonpublished number, 70
Numbers, locating, 29, 59

O

On-line technology, 116, 133–135
   electronic mail (e-mail), 116, 134–135
   Internet, 116, 135
Optional telephone services, 68–71
   additional listing, 70
   automatic callback, 71
   call blocking, 71
   call forwarding, 70
   call pickup, 71
   call trace, 71
   call waiting, 70
   Caller ID, 71
   calling cards, 68
   cellular, 66
   collect calls, 65–66
   conference calls, 68, 71
   delayed call forwarding, 70
   individual call transfer, 71
   nondirectory listed number, 70
   nonpublished number, 70
   person-to-person calls, 66
   phone-number only service, 68
   prepaid phone cards, 68
   selective call waiting, 70
   Speed calling, 70–71

TIME ZONES AND AREA CODES

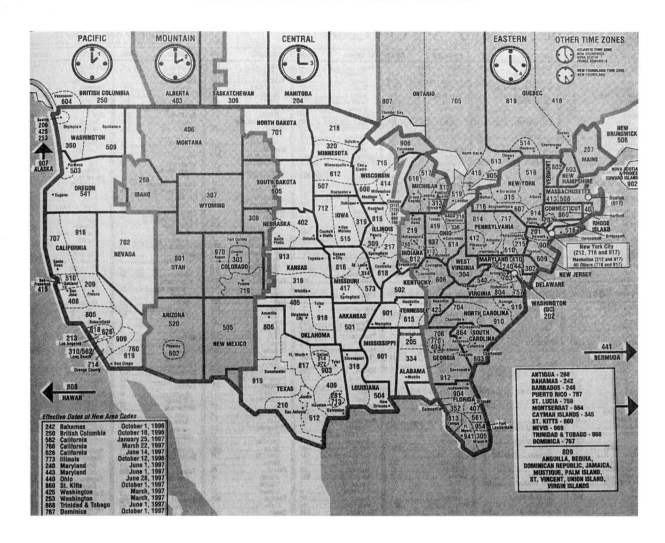